D0292390

THE
COMPUTER
REVOLUTION

THE COMPUTER REVOLUTION

An Economic Perspective

Daniel E. Sichel

BROOKINGS INSTITUTION PRESS
Washington, D.C.

Copyright © 1997 by
THE BROOKINGS INSTITUTION
1775 Massachusetts Avenue, N.W., Washington, D.C. 20036

Library of Congress Cataloging-in-Publication data
Sichel, Daniel E.
    The computer revolution: an economic perspective / Daniel E.
Sichel.
        p. cm.
    Includes bibliographical references and index.
    ISBN 0-8157-7896-1 (cloth : alk. paper). — ISBN 0-8157-7897-X
(paper : al. paper)
    1. Computer industry—United States. 2. Computer service
industry—United States. 3. Computer software industry—United
States. 4. Information technology—United States. 5. United
States—Economic conditions. I. Title.
HD9696.C63U58339   1997
338.4'7004'0973—dc21   97-7425
                                                                             CIP

                          9 8 7 6 5 4 3 2 1

The paper used in this publication meets the minimum requirements of the
American National Standard for Information Sciences—Permanence of Paper
        for Printed Library Materials, ANSI Z39.48-1984

                          Typeset in Sabon

                 Composition by Harlowe Typography, Inc.
                        Cottage City, Maryland

                   Printed by R. R. Donnelley & Sons Co.
                        Harrisonburg, Virginia

Foreword

Iɴ ʀᴇᴄᴇɴᴛ decades, U.S. businesses have spent billions of dollars on information technology, and many commentators have pointed to this computer revolution as a key factor boosting economic growth and productivity. Despite this rapid expansion of computer use, however, the economy's productivity performance has been lackluster. Because increases in productivity are the ultimate source of improved living standards, sluggish productivity growth does not bode well for advances in the nation's economic well-being. Thus, the implications of computerization for economic growth and productivity are a crucial issue for economists, business leaders, and policymakers.

In this book Daniel E. Sichel provides a straightforward guide to the economic issues involved. He reviews the basic facts about computer hardware and software in the economy, explains how information technology contributes to economic growth, and offers a plausible guide on the size of those contributions in recent years. He details what would have to happen for these contributions to pick up substantially in coming years.

Sichel's analysis places limits on the size of the past and future contribution of computers to the overall economy. When compared with the size of the slowdown in productivity growth in the 1970s, the overall impact of computers appears relatively modest, partly because the share of computers in the nation's capital stock is surprisingly small. Consequently, even though information technologies have dramatically affected many individual companies and jobs, caution with respect to macroeconomic effects is in order. The nation can not yet assume that the computer revolution will ensure a huge boost to aggregate productivity growth.

Daniel E. Sichel is a senior economist at the Federal Reserve Board. He completed most of this study as a research associate at the Brookings Institution. He is grateful to many persons who read all or significant parts of the manuscript and provided helpful criticism, suggestions, and comments, including Barry P. Bosworth, Ron Friedmann, William G. Gale, Claudia D. Goldin, Robert J. Gordon, Kalee Krieder, Robert E. Litan, Samuel H. Nelson, Robert P. Parker, George L. Perry, Charles L. Schultze, Jack E. Triplett, and David M. Wessel. Seminar participants at the Brookings Institution, the Bureau of the Census, the Federal Reserve Board, and Washington University also offered many helpful comments. He especially benefited from extensive conversations with Stephen D. Oliner, who coauthored an earlier paper that covered important parts of the material in this study and who shares credit for many of the ideas here. He also appreciates help from Ron Friedmann, Bruce K. MacLaury, and Laurence H. Meyer in setting up the company interviews. The insights, wisdom, and time provided by the interviewees listed in the Appendix greatly benefited the author. Many important parts of the study would not have been possible without the gracious assistance with data given by David Tremblay of the Software Publishers Association, the Bureau of Economic Analysis, and the Bureau of Labor Statistics. The author thanks Kirsten Wallenstein and Derek Douglas for outstanding research assistance and Lisa Guillory for excellent administrative support. Theresa Walker edited the manuscript, Cynthia Iglesias and Helen Kim verified its factual accuracy, Judith Dollenmayer proofread it, and Julia Petrakis prepared the index.

The project was supported by the Edward M. Bernstein Scholars Fund.

The views expressed here are those of the author and should not be ascribed to any of the persons or organizations acknowledged above, to the trustees, officers, or other staff members of the Brookings Institution, or to any other institutions with which the author is affiliated.

Michael H. Armacost
President

May 1997
Washington, D.C.

Contents

Tables

Figures

Boxes

CHAPTER 1

Introduction

$\mathbf{D}$URING THE 1980s and into this decade, U.S. business poured billions of dollars into information technology as computer power exploded and prices plunged.[1] With this surge in computing power, many commentators in the media have pointed to the computer revolution as a key factor in economic growth and productivity. For example, *Business Week* recently told its readers that "the productivity surge of the last two years . . . may reflect the efforts of U.S. companies to finally take full advantage of the huge sums they've spent purchasing information technology."[2] *Forbes ASAP* recently published a piece suggesting, "We may be on the cusp of that long-awaited productivity surge. The explosive growth of PCs, workstations, LANs, WANs, fiber optics, wireless communications and object-oriented software may be completing the new office paradigm."[3]

Others have been more restrained about the productivity impacts of computers, but the view that computers are at the vanguard of an economic revolution is widely held. For example, a U.S. government publication noted, "Computers may be the most profound technology since steam power ignited the Industrial Revolution. Computer technology is altering the form, nature, and future course of the American economy . . . and launching an information highway that is leading to globalization of product and financial markets." A recent report by the National Research Council noted, "As [information technology] becomes less expensive, more portable, better integrated and interconnected, and embedded

1. From 1980 to 1994, the cumulative investment in computers and peripheral equipment in 1987 constant dollars was $630 billion.
2. Michael J. Mandel, "The Digital Juggernaut," *Business Week*, Information Revolution Special Issue, May 18, 1994, p. 23.
3. Michael Rothschild, "The Coming Productivity Surge," *Forbes ASAP*, March 29, 1993, pp. 17–18.

in a wider variety of devices, new applications in these fields and whole new industries . . . are likely to evolve and to have profound effects on industry structures, employment, and economic growth."[4] And rapid technological change is often cited by economists as an important contributor to the widening gap between rich and poor in recent years.[5]

The extensive media coverage of the Information Superhighway suggests that further revolutionary changes are on the way. One study predicted that complete deregulation of telecommunications—to speed the arrival of the Information Highway—would have dramatic economic effects by 2003. The unemployment rate, the study concluded, would be reduced by one-half percentage point, inflation would be held down by almost a full percentage point, the federal budget deficit would decline by $150 billion, and the nation's trade surplus would drop by more than $30 billion.[6]

The basic facts about computer purchases confirm this explosion in computing power at the same time that prices of computing equipment have plummeted. In terms of spending, real purchases by the business sector of computers and peripheral equipment (CPE) grew rapidly over each five-year period between 1970 and the early 1990s and increased much more rapidly than real gross domestic product. Moreover, the total stock of computing equipment in use also surged upward over this period (table 1-1 and figures 1-1, 1-2).

These rapid increases in the use of computers in recent decades were driven partly by plunging prices for computer hardware. Figure 1-3 shows these rapid price declines with an index that takes account of each year's improvement in the performance of computing equipment (see also table 1-1).[7] Because improvements in performance are taken into account, this computer-price index is an estimate of how fast the price-performance ratio has improved for computer and peripheral equipment. These prices have fallen greatly, declining at an average annual pace of

---

4. McConnell (1996, p. 3); and National Research Counci (1994, p. 1).

5. For example, see Bound and Johnson (1992); and Krueger (1992).

6. The study was done in July 1993 by the WEFA Group. See John R. Cranford, "Economy Will Benefit from Deregulation: Question Is, How Much?" Special Report, *The Information Arena, Congressional Quarterly*, supplement to no. 19, May 14, 1994, pp. 33–34.

7. The price index shown for computers is the so-called hedonic index developed by the Bureau of Economic Analysis (BEA), which measures changes in computer prices after accounting for each year's improvement in the performance of computer equipment. For more information about hedonic indexes, see Triplett (1989).

Table 1-1. *Percent Growth in Measures of Information Processing Equipment, 1970–93*

Annual rate, 1987 dollars[a]

Item	1970–75	1975–80	1980–85	1985–90	1990–93
Computers and peripheral equipment					
Real investment	24.1	40.1	33.9	13.3	26.0[b]
Real net capital stock	24.5	33.5	35.4	18.8	20.4[b]
Price deflator	− 18.6	− 15.0	− 14.7	− 11.0	− 16.3[b]
Office, computing, and accounting equipment[c]					
Real investment	10.7	24.0	22.5	9.1	25.8
Real net capital stock	16.2	18.9	26.0	16.7	15.3
Price deflator	− 2.5	− 1.7	− 6.4	− 8.5	− 15.8
Information processing equipment[c]					
Real investment	5.8	14.3	9.0	5.6	13.7
Real net capital stock	8.5	8.9	10.1	9.5	7.1
Price deflator	4.0	4.1	2.3	− 1.8	− 7.5

Source: Based on Oliner and Sichel (1994), using data from U.S. Department of Commerce, Bureau of Economic Analysis. Numbers for the real net stock of computers and peripheral equipment differ slightly from Oliner and Sichel, reflecting the correction of a minor programming error.

a. Average log difference over period shown, multiplied by 100.

b. Values cover period 1990–94.

c. The figures in the table for office, computing, and accounting equipment and for information processing equipment are biased by index-number problems in aggregating up their subcomponents, as described in the Appendix to chapter 3. The figures for computers and peripheral equipment are little affected by such biases.

15.1 percent between 1970 and 1994, compared with an average increase in the overall price level of 5.2 percent a year during the same period.[8]

In the midst of this rapid computerization and high hopes for the future, however, the economy's measured productivity performance has been lackluster. Most often, analysts focus on labor productivity, which measures the amount of real—or inflation-adjusted—output produced per worker or per hour worked.[9] Figure 1-4 plots labor productivity, based on a measure of output that takes into account changes in the econ-

8. The "percent" changes cited are average log differences, multiplied by 100. Some analysts have suggested that BEA's index understates the true pace of decline. Gordon (1990, table 6-12, p. 234) calculates an alternative price index for computers, which is shown in the second column of his table. From 1970 to 1984, log differences of his series imply an annual average decline of 16.9 percent, compared with 14.9 percent for the BEA series, which is shown in the second column of his table 6-11, p. 230. Some authors, including Gordon (pp. 236–37) and Berndt, Griliches, and Rappaport (1993), have noted that prices of personal computers seem to have fallen more rapidly in recent years than did prices of mainframe and minicomputers in the 1970s and early 1980s. Moreover, the transition from mainframes to personal computers may have lowered per-unit costs of computing power in ways that standard price indexes would not capture.

9. Another productivity measure often used by economists is called multifactor productivity. This measure captures output per unit of labor *and* capital inputs.

Figure 1-1. *Growth in Real Computer Investment and Chain-Weighted GDP*

Percent change, annual rate

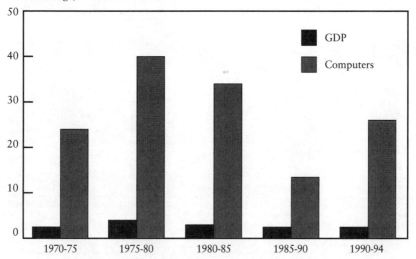

Source: U.S. Department of Commerce (1992) and *Survey of Current Business*, various issues. Figures shown are average annual log differences, multiplied by 100. The computer series is computers and peripheral equipment.

omy's structure over time. As the figure shows, the pace of productivity growth slowed in the early 1970s. To highlight this slowdown, a split trend line is drawn connecting the level of productivity in the peak years 1960, 1973, and 1988.[10] On this measure of productivity, the split trend line indicates that productivity growth averaged 3.0 percent a year through 1973 and then slowed dramatically to 1.1 percent annually thereafter.

Figure 1-5 shows that—despite an improvement in productivity growth in the early 1990s—productivity had just managed to rise back up to its lackluster trend by 1995. And, as forcefully argued by Robert Gordon, the evidence suggests that this pickup in growth in the early 1990s reflects a cyclical bounceback from the pause before and during the 1990–91 recession.[11] Thus, despite rapid computerization, productivity growth has not broken out from the sluggish trend that has per-

10. These years were chosen to connect peaks in the productivity cycle. The years 1960 and 1973 correspond to business cycle peaks designated by the National Bureau of Economic Research. The year 1988 comes before the business cycle peak in 1990 because productivity growth began to slow notably in 1989.

11. Gordon (1993).

Figure 1-2. *Growth in Real Net Stock of Computer and Peripheral Equipment, 1971–95*

Percent change, annual rate

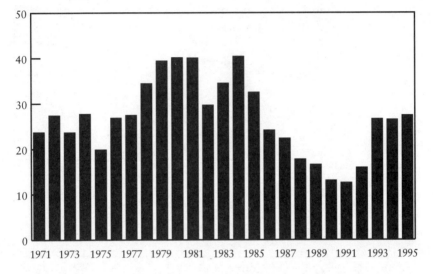

Source: Based on Oliner and Sichel (1994) calculations with BEA investment data and weights, extended to 1994 and 1995 as described in the Appendix to chapter 3. Real net stock measured in 1987 constant dollars. Figures shown are annual log differences multiplied by 100. Figures differ slightly from Oliner and Sichel, reflecting correction of minor programming error.

sisted since the early 1970s.[12] Because increases in productivity are the ultimate source of improvements in living standards, a continuation of sluggish productivity growth would not bode well for future advances in the nation's economic well-being.

12. In January of 1996, the Bureau of Economic Analysis (BEA) began featuring chain-weight measures of real output that take account of changes in the economy's structure over time. These measures chain together aggregation weights from different years, rather than using a single year's weights as in the constant-dollar measures. Before the introduction of the chain-weight measures, the conventional constant-dollar measures published by BEA were subject to significant biases that confounded analysis of productivity growth over time. This bias arose because the conventional measure was adjusted for inflation by setting the price of each item of output to its 1987 price. But by 1994 relative prices had changed substantially from their 1987 level, and using the out-of-date prices generated biases. For example, computers are one of the fastest-growing components of GDP and a component whose price has fallen rapidly. Using the much-too-high 1987 price for computers in later years overweights their importance in GDP, thereby generating a sizable upward bias in real GDP growth. Because of this upward bias, the old constant-dollar measures of productivity had risen well above the trend line depicted in figures 1-4 and 1-5, leading some observers to hold out hope that productivity growth had broken out of its sluggish trend. For more detail on chain-weighted indexes, see *Survey of Current Business*, April and November 1992, and *Economic Report of the President, 1995*, p. 97.

Figure 1-3. *Computer Prices and the Overall Price Level, 1970–94 (Index Level)*

Log index points

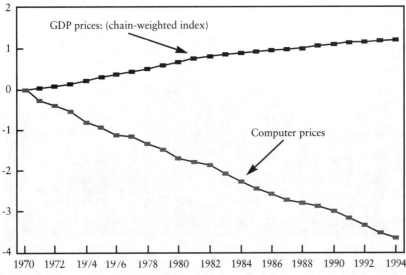

Source: U.S. Department of Commerce (1992); and *Survey of Current Business*, various issues.

Thus, how much computerization translates into economic growth and productivity is crucial for all concerned with the nation's economic well-being. The nation is beginning to embark on a serious effort to develop an Information Superhighway. The business sector continues to deploy increasingly powerful computer hardware and software, at the same time that more and more households are buying computers and hooking up to the Internet. If large gains in productivity are realized from these investments, then the prospects for growth of productivity and living standards in the future could brighten significantly. If information technology is not a magic bullet, however, then future productivity gains would have to come about through more traditional means, including increases in saving and investment, intensified research and development, improved education and training, and managerial advances. For these reasons, policymakers, business managers, and the general public must have realistic expectations about how great an aggregate economic boost information technology might impel.

In terms of assessing the pace of increase in living standards, an additional complication has gained attention recently. Namely the difficul-

Figure 1-4. *Actual and Trend Labor Productivity, 1960–95*[a]

Nonfarm business, 1960–95, chain weighted, 1992=100

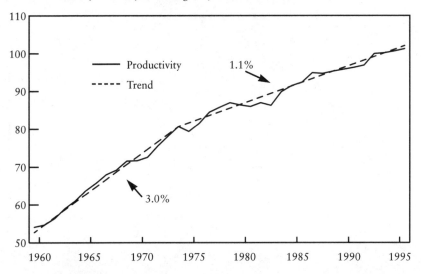

Source: Nonfarm business output per hour for all persons from U.S. Department of Labor, Bureau of Labor Statistics, Productivity and Cost Data.

a. Trend based on author's calculation. Trends drawn through 1960, 1973, and 1988, with growth rates shown based on average log differences.

ties of accurately measuring economic performance. Although economists have grappled with measurement issues for a long time, these issues have received welcome public attention recently, spurred in part by the Boskin Commission report on the accuracy of the Consumer Price Index (CPI). The Boskin Commission emphasized the impact of potential mismeasurement in the CPI on indexation of government spending and tax programs. However, these measurement issues are also important for assessing links between information technology and economic performance.[13]

This book does not present new research on the links between computers and economic growth, but rather—in as nontechnical a manner as possible—offers an economic perspective on the principal issues. This book reviews the basic facts about computer hardware and software in the economy, identifies the channels through which information technology contributes to economic growth, provides a plausible guide to the size of those contributions in recent years, and details what would have

13. Boskin Commission (1996). Michael J. Boskin was chairman of the Advisory Commission to Study the Price Index. Other members included Ellen R. Dulberger, Robert J. Gordon, Zvi Griliches, and Dale Jorgenson.

Figure 1-5. *Actual and Trend Labor Productivity, 1988–95*[a]

Nonfarm business, 1988–95, chain weighted, 1992=100

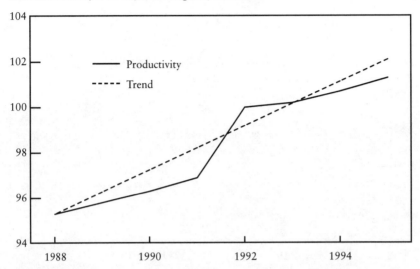

Source: Nonfarm labor productivity for all persons from U.S. Department of Labor, Bureau of Labor Statistics.
a. Trend based on author's calculation. Trend drawn through 1973 and 1988, with growth rates calculated as average log differences.

to happen for these contributions to pick up substantially in coming years. The historical analysis sheds more light on the role of computers in the economy and on recent media coverage of the computer revolution.

Scope and Methodology

This study focuses on computing equipment used primarily in office settings in the business sector, including personal computers, workstations, minicomputers, servers, mainframes, and related equipment. A broader focus than computing equipment could, of course, be taken. For example, the entire microelectronics revolution could be considered, including all products that contain semiconductors.[14] Another approach

14. The difficulties of separating and measuring the output of computers are daunting; separating and measuring the contribution of all semiconductors to economic growth and productivity may be an order of magnitude more challenging. Even if the focus could be expanded in this way to cover all semiconductors, the results might not be that different than for computers. As reported in OECD (1994, pp. 33–35), the worldwide semiconductor

would span all technologies used for gathering, processing, and transmitting information.[15] These broader purviews are of interest, but they are not my primary focus. Most analysts studying the computer paradox have concentrated on computers for three reasons. For one thing, they believe that computers are "special" and different from other inventions in important ways, namely, in their ability to process information in ways that approximate human thought and intelligence. Second, computers are ubiquitous in the modern world. And third, at least historically, computers have been the most technologically dynamic piece of broader classifications of information-processing equipment.

Because most discussions of productivity focus on the business sector, this study emphasizes computers used in the workplace rather than in the home. Second, as shown in chapter 3 and noted by many authors, most computers used in the economy are in the service sector.[16] Much of this equipment is office-based, just as much of the computing equipment used outside the service sector—such as in a manufacturing company— also is used in office settings. Thus, this study emphasizes office-based computing equipment. Besides hardware, however, this study considers software and computer-related labor, which is crucial because hardware must be combined with software and labor inputs to be used effectively.

In methodology, this book primarily focuses on the links between information technology and overall economic growth at the aggregate level. This approach will not answer questions about whether or not a company is getting its money's worth from a particular application of computers, but it can provide important insights into their effects on economic growth in the economy as a whole. This aggregate analysis is supplemented by information obtained from focused interviews with seven service-sector companies in the United States, ranging from a 65-person engineering consulting firm to a $13-billion-a-year retailer with about 30,000 employees. Although the anecdotal evidence gained from these interviews is not conclusive in itself, it does highlight and make concrete many of the issues that emerge in the more aggregate analysis. Material from the interviews appears in boxes throughout the book; the companies and interviews are described in the Appendix.

---

market is about one-sixth the size of the worldwide computer market. About half of all semiconductors produced are used in the computer industry.

15. See Roach (1991); and Lau and Tokutsu (1992) for analyses that take a broader focus.

16. For example, see Roach (1991); and Griliches (1994, pp. 11–12).

Summary

Several themes emerge from the analysis, as follows.

Computer Hardware and Recent Economic Growth

As shown in chapter 3, computer hardware—including computers and related peripheral equipment—makes up only about 2 percent of the nation's capital stock; that is, computers constitute a small share of the inputs used to produce goods and services in the U.S. economy. In large part, the capital share of computer hardware has remained so small because computers become obsolete so rapidly; as fast as new machines come in the front door, old machines are carted out the back door. Because of this small share, computer hardware's contribution to overall economic growth is limited, even if hardware were to earn a higher return than other investments companies might make. As estimated in chapter 4, the real output of the nonfarm business sector increased by 2.0 percent annually between 1987 and 1993. Computer hardware is estimated to have contributed 0.15 percentage point to this growth on the assumption that computers earn a competitive rate of return.

Software and Computer-Related Labor Inputs

As emphasized throughout this book, all tasks done with a computer require a combination of hardware, software, and labor inputs. Thus, in an assessment of the computer revolution, the appropriate focus of analysis is computing services—consisting of hardware, software and computer-related labor—not just computer hardware. Broadening the focus in this way roughly doubles the contribution of hardware just cited to 0.3 percentage point a year. Although such a contribution would cumulate to billions of dollars over time, it remains modest when compared with the slowdown in productivity in the early 1970s. Moreover, about half of computing services' contribution to growth just goes to cover costs of depreciation and obsolescence of computer hardware and software, considerably diminishing the amount that can contribute to an improvement in the nation's economic well-being.

Computing Services and Future Growth

Extending the growth-accounting framework into the future reveals that continued rapid growth in the stock of computer hardware and software is not enough, in and of itself, to generate a substantial pickup in the contribution of computing services to output growth. To get a big pickup, the return earned by computer hardware and software must surge in coming years. Although such a surge is certainly a possibility, there are reasons to doubt that such a surge is yet under way.

Software and the National Income and Product Accounts (GDP Accounts)

At this time, software is only partially included in the GDP Accounts. Rough estimates suggest that counting purchases of software just like investments in computer hardware would have boosted the growth rate of real business investment in equipment by as much as three-fourths of a percentage point from 1991 to 1993. For overall GDP, however, more complete coverage of software in the accounts has a relatively modest impact. Although real GDP is higher once software's coverage is expanded, software's share of GDP is just too small to have much impact on overall GDP growth rates. For real GDP, more complete coverage of software is estimated to have boosted real GDP growth by about 0.1 percentage point a year from 1991 to 1993, according to rough calculations.

Mismeasurement, Computers, and Productivity Growth

Because so much of the output generated by computers is intangible, many analysts have suggested that if measurement tools were better, a more substantial contribution of computers to output growth would be evident. My analysis casts doubt on this argument in three ways. First, computers make up a small share of all inputs to the economy so that even if their output were substantially undermeasured, computer hardware's true contribution to output growth would still be modest.

Second, the final-demand share of the difficult-to-measure services produced by computers is small. This share is small because so many of the services produced by computers are purchased by other companies as inputs, which are not directly counted in GDP to avoid double counting. For example, financial services accounted for just 4.6 percent of GDP in 1994, after eliminating double counting. Thus, if a computer-driven explosion in the productivity of financial services has occurred, its impact on the economy as a whole would be limited.

Third, little evidence suggests that the measurement gap between actual output growth and measured output growth has increased greatly in recent years. If computers are pushing actual output growth far above measured output growth, then this measurement gap should have become larger as computer use increased. Although it is extremely difficult to assess the impact of measurement error, there are reasons to doubt that the measurement gap has opened up dramatically in the past decade. Most recently, the Boskin Commission report examined measurement error in the nation's economic statistics, particularly the CPI. While that report found evidence of substantial mismeasurement in the CPI, the report did not argue that the amount of mismeasurement has increased significantly over time.

Continuities between Current and Past Developments in Information Technology

Important continuities exist between current and past developments in information technology. Businesses applied information technology to coordination problems long before desktop computing arrived through the use of typewriters, telegraphs, telephones, calculating and tabulating machines, and, starting in the 1950s, mainframe computers. In these earlier periods, office-automation equipment underwent rapid innovation, and the companies that produced this equipment were major players in the economy. The economy's information intensity has been on an uptrend for more than one hundred and fifty years.

Optimism in Popular Commentary

Much recent media coverage of the computer revolution has been quite upbeat. Since the late 1950s, however, observers in the business press have often proclaimed optimistically that recent problems in getting full value from computers had largely been overcome and that a surge was just around the corner. Perhaps the optimists are right this time. But then again, perhaps this optimism should be discounted, since this genre of commentary on the computer revolution has been around for years.

Chapter Outline

Chapter 2 presents an economic framework for assessing the links between computing services and economic growth. In light of that framework, it also discusses the computer paradox—the puzzle about why productivity growth has remained sluggish in the midst of rapid computerization. This chapter is the most technical of the book, although much of the technical material appears in appendixes. Chapter 3 recounts the basic facts about computer hardware and software in the U.S. economy and provides rough estimates of how the National Income Accounts would change if software were included more comprehensively. Chapter 4 uses the economic framework from chapter 2, along with the data from chapter 3, to provide rough estimates of the contribution of computing services to overall economic growth in recent years. It also looks ahead to assess what must occur if this contribution is to increase significantly in the future. Finally, chapter 5 provides some historical perspective on the computer revolution and media coverage of that revolution and includes a brief conclusion.

CHAPTER 2

The Economics of the Computer Revolution

T HIS CHAPTER describes an analytic framework, pioneered by Edward Denison and referred to as neoclassical, for assessing the role of computers in economic growth.[1] By imposing analytic rigor, this framework highlights the crucial links that affect the size of this role. In addition, the framework sheds light on the productivity paradox, the puzzle over why productivity growth has remained sluggish in the midst of rapid computerization.

A Framework for Linking Computers and Economic Growth

The intuition for Denison's framework is straightforward, although the mechanics can be somewhat complicated. The basic intuition goes as follows. Suppose the contribution of computers to output growth between two periods is to be calculated. In any period, the contribution of computers to overall income will depend on the quantity of computers in use and the return earned by them. If the quantity and average return are known, then multiplying them together yields the income flow from computers in any period. (The neoclassical framework assumes that, on the margin of the last dollar invested, firms earn the same competitive rate of return on computers as on other investments.) These income flows can be compared across periods to assess the increase in the income flow generated by computers. Scaled by the size of the economy, these calculations can show the contribution of computers to overall economic growth. Obviously, this framework has some limitations and requires many assumptions about how the economy functions. Therefore, extensions to the neoclassical framework are also considered.

---

1. For example, see Denison (1985).

Figure 2-1. *Computer Prices and Real Investment, 1961–94*
Computer and Peripheral Equipment

Price index

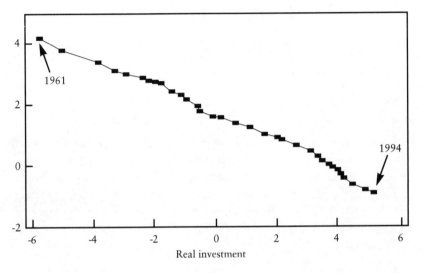

Real investment

Source: Investment in 1987 dollars and price deflator from U.S. Department of Commerce (1992); and *Survey of Current Business*, various issues. Series plotted are natural logarithms of actual series.

Supply and Demand

A simple supply and demand framework for computers highlights the basic economics underlying the rapid expansion in computer use. The single factor that most drives the rapid expansion in computer spending is the rapid and relentless decline in price. Figure 2-1 shows the relationship between prices and real investment for computers and peripheral equipment from 1961 to 1994. Because prices have fallen while real investment has risen every year, each box moving from left to right represents the next year in sequence. Clearly, as prices have dropped each year, purchases have climbed further upward.

For the most part, the rapid decline in computer prices reflects technological progress in the manufacture of computers, or more accurately, technological progress in the components going into computers, including microprocessors, memory, disk drives, and so on.[2] Because the decline

2. Kenneth Flamm has written extensively about the development of computers. See Flamm (1987, 1988).

Figure 2-2. *Supply and Demand for Computers: A Conceptual View*

Price

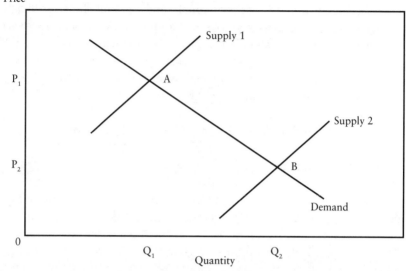

in computer prices has been largely driven by developments on the supply side, it is plausible—at least as a rough approximation—that the line in figure 2-1 represents a demand curve, while each box on the line represents an intersection with a supply curve that keeps shifting downward over time.[3]

If this view is accepted, then a simple supply-demand framework provides a natural vehicle for describing the effects of computers on the economy. Figure 2-2 shows a stylized version of figure 2-1, with the supply curves drawn in. Consider a shift in the supply curve from Supply 1 to Supply 2, inducing a shift from the point labeled A to B. Next I describe the formulas needed to quantify the impact of just such a shift on total income or output.[4]

3. Without a doubt, the demand curve for computers has shifted outward during the period shown in figure 2-1, as incomes have grown and as new generations of computers have been introduced. Nevertheless, the prime driving force has been the plunge in the price of hardware as the supply curve has shifted out.

4. The terms *income* and *output* will be used interchangeably throughout this chapter and elsewhere in the book. Income refers to the payments made to factors of production to produce output, including wages paid to labor and interest and dividends paid to capital. Output refers to the total value of goods and services produced by these factors of production. Under the usual rules of income accounting, the income received by factors of production equals the value of what is produced. Hence, these terms can be used interchangeably.

The Neoclassical Framework

In the highly stylized world of supply and demand shown in figure 2-2, assume that businesses always make optimal investment decisions and that all types of capital earn the same competitive return at the margin. Economists refer to such a world as neoclassical. This neoclassical model is useful because it provides a simple framework for assessing the impact of computers on output that captures the influence of basic economic forces.

Consider point A in figure 2-2, the intersection of the demand curve and Supply 1. In this stylized neoclassical world, this intersection represents an equilibrium at which every business is buying the ideal amount of computing equipment, given the price. That is, for each potential additional purchase of computers or other investments, firms are setting their capital budgets to equalize returns on these additional investments at the cost of capital.[5] If returns were not equalized at the cost of capital, then firms would be better off by spending more on investments that had returns higher than the cost of capital and less on investments with returns lower than the cost of capital.

Now, suppose technological improvement in semiconductors shifts the supply curve out to Supply 2 in figure 2-2. As the price falls and it becomes profitable to deploy computers for applications further down the demand curve, the quantity of computer purchases rises from Q_1 to the new optimal level of purchases Q_2. How much would the nation's income or output increase?

In the neoclassical framework, computers earn a competitive return. For now, assume that there are no taxes, depreciation, market frictions, or changes in relative prices. Then the increment to income would equal the increase in the stock of computers multiplied by the rate of return earned by this equipment. More specifically, call the competitive return r_{COMP} and let K_1 be the total stock of computers associated with purchases of Q_1.[6] Similarly, let K_2 be the higher total capital stock associated with purchases Q_2. Between point A and B, the increment to the stock of computers would equal $K_2 - K_1$. In this neoclassical world, the return on that increment would be r_{COMP}, and the boost to output would be the

---

5. With taxes and depreciation, optimizing firms would equalize returns net of these expenses.

6. Without depreciation or obsolescence, the stock of computers would be the accumulation of all past purchases; with depreciation and obsolescence, this stock is reduced each year by the amount of depreciation and obsolescence.

increase in the stock of computers multiplied by the competitive rate of return. Thus, the shift from Supply 1 to Supply 2 would boost output by:

(2-1) Neoclassical boost to output from computers

$$= r_{COMP} (K_2 - K_1).$$

As shown in the Appendix to this chapter, equation 2-1 can be transformed to show the neoclassical contribution of computers to output *growth*, rather than the boost to the level of output. By switching to growth rates, the term for the increment to the capital stock $(K_2 - K_1)$ becomes the growth rate of the capital stock denoted by $\dot{K}_C$, while the term for the rate of return earned by computers (r_{COMP}) becomes the share of total income generated by computers (s_C). More specifically,

(2-2) Neoclassical computer contribution to real output growth

$$= s_C \dot{K}_C.$$

Estimates of the contribution in equation 2-2 are discussed in chapter 4. To improve intuition now, however, it is useful to take a moment to examine the income share, s_C, in more detail.

The Income Share and the Competitive Rate of Return

The share of income generated by computers is the ratio of the nominal income flow generated by computers to total nominal income. And the income flow from computers equals the nominal stock of computers multiplied by the gross rate of return earned by computers. More specifically,

income share of computers $= s_C$

(2-3) $=$ (income flow) / (total income)

$=$ (gross rate of return) × (nominal stock of computers)

/ (total income).

In the earlier discussion, the competitive rate of return earned by computers was r_{COMP}, the same return earned by other investments. While r_{COMP} captures the return in a world without depreciation, the total or gross return that a firm expects to earn on a capital investment must also cover the costs of depreciation or gradual loss in value as an asset wears out or becomes obsolete (d). Thus, the gross return earned by computers must be

(2-4) gross rate of return = (competitive net return) + depreciation

$$= r_{COMP} + d.$$

Estimates of the terms of equation 2-4 can be taken from Oliner and Sichel.[7] For the net rate of return (r_{COMP}), they used data from the Bureau of Labor Statistics to estimate that the competitive rate of return to all nonresidential equipment and structures averaged about 12 percent from 1970 to 1992, in nominal terms. In addition, they estimated, based on data from the Bureau of Economic Analysis, that the depreciation rate for computers (d) averaged 25 percent over this period; that is, computers lose about 25 percent of their value each year. Adding together the net competitive return and the depreciation rate yields a gross return ($r_{COMP} + d$) of 37 percent.

Take note of this large gross return. Because computers become obsolete so rapidly, the gross return earned by computers must be about 37 percent to cover these large obsolescence costs while still providing a competitive return net of depreciation. Reports of large returns earned by computing equipment are perfectly consistent with computers earning a competitive return net of depreciation. If computers did not earn a hefty return, their owners would be losing money after accounting for the rapid obsolescence of the machines. Moreover, note the composition of the gross return. Depreciation accounts for two-thirds of the gross return, while the competitive return back to the firm after covering depreciation costs is just one-third of the gross return.

The gross rate of return is only one piece of the income share; the stock of computers in the economy will matter as well. Although the focus will expand later to include computer software and labor inputs as well, consider the income share of computer hardware alone as an illustrative example. To obtain the income share for computer hardware (s_C), the large gross return of 37 percent is multiplied by the nominal stock of computers and then divided by total nominal income. In 1992 the nominal stock of computers and peripheral equipment was $95.9 billion. Multiplying by 0.37 for the gross rate of return implies that the income flow from computers was roughly $35.5 billion [(= $95.9 billion) ×

---

7. Oliner and Sichel (1994, pp. 283–85).

(0.37)]. While a large figure, this income flow was just 0.8 percent of total nominal income of $4,494.4 billion in 1992.[8] That is, if computer hardware earned a competitive return, it accounted for only 0.8 percent of all income generated in the economy in 1992 because computers are so small compared with the size of the overall economy. When estimates of the contribution of computer hardware to output growth are presented in chapter 4, this small income share will place limits on the contribution of computer hardware.

Two Important Implications

By imposing analytic rigor, this framework highlights two critical points for understanding the impact of computers on the economy. First, as computer prices fall over time, computers will be applied to tasks that have lower payoffs; in the language of economics, the marginal product of computers will decline over time. Second, the neoclassical framework sharpens our understanding of the conditions necessary to get a pickup in output growth.

Start with the first point about marginal products. Almost every discussion of the productivity payoff of computers begins with the observation that a dollar today buys so much more computing power than in past years, and sometimes this observation is taken to imply that computers must be making a large contribution to productivity. Although this argument has obvious merit, the neoclassical framework highlights a critical point that affects the force of the argument. Namely, that as prices of computers decline, they are often used for applications that have lower payoffs.[9] In the simple supply and demand world of figure 2-2, point A has a very important property. At point A, computers have been deployed to every application for which it is profitable to do so. There are, of course, additional computer applications further down the demand curve. But, at point A computers are still too expensive to be worth using for these applications.

As the price falls from P_1 to P_2, businesses now go ahead and deploy computers for those applications that were not profitable when the price

8. Nominal capital stock for CPE is based on the author's calculations using the procedure described in Oliner and Sichel (1994). Nominal output is nonfarm business less housing from *Survey of Current Business*, vol. 74 (July 1994), p. 56, table 1-7.

9. Jack Triplett made this point in his comment on Oliner and Sichel (1994, pp. 323–24).

of computers was still P_1. Again, putting this concept into the language of economics, firms buy computers until the marginal product from the additional computers just equals the marginal cost of an additional unit. As the cost or price of computers falls, it is profitable for companies to deploy computers for activities that have a lower marginal product.

This point bears emphasis. A dollar today buys more computer power than a quarter of a century earlier, but that computer power may well be deployed for an activity that has a much lower marginal product or payoff than twenty-five years earlier. For example, the average general purpose mainframe computer system shipped in 1970 had a price tag in excess of $800,000—or more than $2.8 million in 1994 dollars.[10] But at such a price, mainframes were deployed only for high-level applications, such as controlling an Apollo moonshot, not for more mundane applications like word processing. Today, many Pentium computers are used extensively for word processing because their price has fallen far enough.[11] Moreover, mainframe computers in the 1970s were run with time-sharing systems to ensure maximum use of the machine's processing power and minimize the machine's idle time. In contrast, many personal computers today are used intermittently and stand idle much of the time. Thus, when one considers how much more computing power a dollar buys today than some years ago, one must remember that today's marginal computer dollar may be going to a lower payoff activity and to a machine that is less heavily utilized.

As for changes in tasks and processes over time, the focused interviews provide some specific examples, as described in box 2-1. Although respondents generally did not see these shifts in tasks through a neoclassical prism, the neoclassical framework provides a natural interpretation of the respondents' examples. Besides shifts in tasks performed by computers, the neoclassical framework could be extended to consider the mix of workers performing various tasks as computer prices fall. Not surprisingly, the focused interviews point to a tendency for low-skill clerical jobs to disappear and for remaining support staff positions to become more challenging and demanding. These changes are described in box 2-2.

10. Price data for mainframe system in 1970 from Phister (1979, pp. 251–52). To convert this to 1994 dollars, the GDP deflator from the *Economic Report of the President, 1995*, p. 278, was used.

11. E-mail is another interesting example. As e-mail has virtually become a free good for many people, "junk" e-mail has proliferated.

The second important point emerging from the neoclassical framework is the conditions necessary to get a pickup in output growth. In this framework, a decline in the price of computers leads to an expansion in their use and a boost to the level of output. Thus, steady declines in computer prices and steady increases in the use of computers would lead to steady rates of output growth. To generate faster rates of output growth, the pace of price decline or the pace of increase in computer use has to pick up.

This last point is important, and a misunderstanding could lead observers astray. For example, commentators will sometimes note that computer prices fell rapidly in the past five years and then infer that output growth should have picked up in the past five years. In the neoclassical framework, however, rapid declines in computer prices would not be enough to generate faster output growth. To generate faster output growth, computer prices would have had to decline more rapidly in the past five years than in earlier periods. And, as seen earlier in figure 1-3 and table 1-1, the pace of decline in prices for computers and peripheral equipment has been remarkably stable.[12]

This levels-versus-growth-rates distinction also affects the interpretation of anecdotal evidence. Casual observers will often cite a particular advance in computer technology—such as the advent of CD ROMs for personal computers—and then infer that this innovation should have led to faster output growth. As the framework here highlights, however, a steady pace of innovations would lead to steady output growth, just as would a steady decline in prices. Achieving faster output growth would require a pickup in the pace of innovation. Thus, as far as output *growth* is concerned, the right question to ask is not whether CD ROMs represent

---

12. As table 1-1 and figure 1-3 showed, the pace of decline in the deflator for CPE has not increased over time. However, as pointed out by Oliner and Sichel (1994, p. 278), focusing on the price deflator for the broader category of office, computing, and accounting equipment (OCA) rather than the deflator for computers and peripheral equipment (CPE) might falsely lead to a contrary conclusion. As shown in table 1-1, the pace of decline in the OCA deflator does become more rapid in later periods, from which the inference might be drawn that the pace of technical advance has sped up. In fact, this apparent acceleration reflects the compositional shift within OCA, rather than a pickup in the pace of advance for computers. As CPE accounted for a larger and larger share of the OCA measure, the deflator for OCA places a heavier weight on the CPE component whose price is falling much faster than other parts of OCA. As the CPE weight increases over time, the OCA deflator declines more rapidly over time. This accelerating decline does not reflect a faster pace of technological advance, but rather just a shift in composition within the OCA aggregate.

Box 2-1. *Information Technology and Changes in Tasks and Processes*

Most of the companies interviewed indicated that a shift has occurred in the types of tasks and processes that have been the focus of new information technology efforts. The larger companies usually described this change as a shift from automating tasks that were already being done to doing completely new things with information technology, especially things that "touch" the customer. The following quotes are representative, coming from three of the larger mainframe-using companies:

> Historically, in a mainframe environment we always looked at what we could automate. What could be done more efficiently or effectively with the computer. But over time, particularly in the past five years, [we have focused more on] what we can do to create more value for [our customers] and on what is more visible to [our customers.]

> Historically, [our efforts with information technology] have been very cost reduction focused . . . Today, with more affordable technology, we're on the brink of using technology to increase margins and [revenues] . . . With low-level functionality in place, we can move up the food chain in terms of applications to begin to tailor [our products] to meet the needs of specific [market segments.]

> Think of a continuum from work that is 100 percent labor intensive to work that is 100 percent thinking intensive . . . In the early days, we were [applying technology] to improve the productivity of people doing labor intensive tasks. Now, we're trying to apply technology further on the continuum toward thinking-intensive tasks—planning, design, analysis, and decisionmaking.

Although the smaller companies have been relying on computer-related information technology for a shorter length of time, similar shifts were described. Ross and Baruzzini's Maurice Garoutte nicely summed up this view:

The key word is automate. Automation means take a task that is done a particular way and do the same task automatically. That's good. I salute that. . . . Five years ago, we were automating things that we were already doing. . . . Now, we're moving beyond automation. Not just automating things that we were [already] doing, but doing new things that could not have been done the old way.

It would be easy to infer from these observations that companies now must be getting a bigger productivity bang for their computer buck than in the past, as computers are deployed for a wider and wider range of activities. This inference could be true, and qualitative evidence from interviews can neither prove nor disprove its verity. The neoclassical framework described above would, however, put a different interpretation on these changes in the growing range of tasks to which information technology is being applied.

Figure 2-2 shows a supply curve that continued to shift downward along a demand curve as performance-price ratios improved. This downward shift pushes firms further out on their demand curves for information technology, as the price falls. Put another way, the price declines make it feasible for companies to apply information technology to more and more tasks. Five years ago, these tasks did not have a high enough payoff to be worth undertaking, given the costs of technology at that time. But today, at much lower prices for computing services, these activities are worth doing.

Under this interpretation, the fact that companies are now using information technology for new tasks would not necessarily imply larger productivity payoffs but rather might represent a continuing application of information technology to projects further out the demand curve as prices fall further and further.

Box 2-2. *Information Technology and Changes in Support Staff*

Although experiences at specific companies differed, every company linked some changes in their employment mix to information technology. Most of theses changes affected support staff. In general, low-skilled clerical jobs have disappeared, while remaining support staff positions have become more challenging and demanding.

Not surprisingly, every company indicated that they have fewer secretaries and clerical support staff now than five or ten years ago as a result of office automation. For example, both law firms indicated that they have mostly moved from a ratio of one secretary per lawyer to one secretary per two lawyers. Target Stores indicated that they have half as many secretaries as five years ago and have eliminated a host of keypunch positions. Vanguard and St. Paul's Personal and Business Insurance indicated that clerical workers doing straight data entry are disappearing.

Interestingly, some of these companies also indicated that the jobs done by remaining support staff have been upskilled; for example, remaining secretaries have more challenging (and by some reports more satisfying) jobs. John Hamilton, managing partner at Hale and Dorr, said, "The morale of our support staff is much better than ten years ago because the opportunity for growth is so much greater and the work is less tedious." Bill Lake, at Wilmer, Cutler, and Pickering, echoed the same thought, "The ratio of secretaries to lawyers has gone down substantially, and I think they have more satisfying jobs than they did before." At Ross and Baruzzini, Carl Hauck put it, "[These new technologies] have not led to fewer support staff, but their functions have changed and they are tending to do more creative work."

a leap forward, but rather whether CD ROMs represent a bigger leap forward than innovations in earlier years.

Box 2-3 provides further perspective on whether the pace of progress has picked up, reporting evidence on this point from the focused interviews. Although such anecdotes are not definitive, the interviews suggested that larger companies have not tended to see a pickup in the pace of progress on the information-technology front, but that smaller firms have perceived an acceleration.

Supernormal Returns and Welfare Effects

This section considers extensions to the basic economic framework just described. The first extension examines how the basic framework changes if companies earn better than a competitive, or neoclassical, return on computers. The second and third extensions shift the focus from economic growth to measures of economic welfare or well-being.

Supernormal Returns

Many analysts have raised questions about the neoclassical assumption that computers earn the same return as other capital investments.[13] If computers are special and earn a better return than other investments, then the static analysis in figure 2-2 could miss much of what is important. There are two ways in which computing equipment might earn a supernormal return.

First, private returns to computer investment might exceed competitive rates. In a dynamic setting, companies may identify new profit opportunities and earn a better-than-competitive return by moving faster than their competitors during periods of dynamic disequilibrium. Because information technology often plays a critical role in the exploitation of these opportunities—enabling reorganization, reengineering, and streamlining throughout a business—the first companies out of the gate may earn a supernormal return on their computer investments until the competition catches up.[14]

Second, the benefits of computer investments might spill over and benefit workers or other businesses by raising the overall level of technical sophistication in the economy. That is, the social return to computers might exceed the private return because of externalities not captured by the firm making the investment.

Suppose that for one of these two reasons computing equipment earned a supernormal return at point A and at point B in figure 2-2. Then, the impact of computers on the aggregate economy will be larger than that captured through the neoclassical channel. To see this, let r_{SUPER}

---

13. For general discussion of supernormal returns on computers and other capital investments, see Brynjolfsson and Hitt (1996); DeLong and Summers (1991, 1992); Krueger (1993); Lichtenberg (1993); and Romer (1987).

14. Federal Express is an often-mentioned example. See also *Business Week* (1994); and David Hage and Linda Grant, "How to Make America Work," *U.S. News and World Report*, December 6, 1993, for more examples.

Box 2-3. *Has the Pace of Productivity Progress from Information Technology Picked Up?*

In the interviews, many questions were asked about the pace of progress and productivity payoffs from information technology and whether they had picked up in recent years. To some extent, answers differed between the large and the small companies.

Many of the mainframe users emphasized that progress has come as a continual series of upward steps and has appeared in lumpy chunks. In response to a question about the pace of progress over the past ten years, the following answers—from two different companies using mainframes—were typical:

"I don't see abrupt discontinuities, but rather gradual improvement." Added a colleague, "I see that too, but you will see spurts."

We evolved with continual improvements, but there were discrete steps with each major development effort. The early 1980s was one step . . . and the early 1990s is another.

The opportunity for productivity increases grows incrementally, but the ability to learn and apply new things happens in chunks.

[One large development project brought up to speed in the late 1980s] was a real milestone. But since then, our progress from a mainframe perspective or from a PC perspective has been incremental. We have not done another quantum leap.

Respondents at one of the other mainframe-using companies gave similar answers but also expressed a belief that the pace of progress is about to speed up: "For the last seven years, improvements were incremental." Added a colleague, "Expectations for progress are getting bigger [now, and] I think we're starting to see a little bit of a breakout."

The companies that were only running desktop networks have been using computer-related information technology for a much shorter period of time, never relying on mainframe systems. These three smaller companies (the two law firms and the engineering company) also described the pace of productivity improvement associated with information technology as a series of steps and plateaus. At these companies, however, respondents were much more likely to indicate that the pace of progress has picked up in recent years.

Michael Klein, comanaging partner at Wilmer, Cutler, and Pickering, expressed this view as, "It's bumpy and there are spurts as new avenues open up. [Our system is] constantly getting a little better, but the increments are relatively small . . . [Overall,] it's sped up somewhat. E-mail, CD-ROM [libraries of legal material], and document management are all just beginning." John Hamilton, of Hale and Dorr, put it, "It's a series of breakthroughs with one cascading on top of another . . . the frequency of breakthroughs is much more rapid [now] because you don't have the resistance from people in the organization." Respondents at Ross and Baruzzini also pointed to a speedup in recent years. As Carl Hauck, president of the Missouri Division of the engineering firm, put it, "We've seen more changes in the last two years in this office than the previous trend . . . the hardware and software have gotten to a point where it is better to do it the new way."

Putting together the responses from the larger and smaller companies yields a mixed answer to the question whether the pace of productivity improvement has picked up in recent years. The mainframe users—with their longer perspective on the development and application of information technology—saw the additional deployment of personal computers as another step in a long sequence of steps. In general, they did not see recent developments as a complete break from the past. In contrast, the smaller companies—whose first major exposure to computer-related information technology came more recently through their desktop networks—appear to have experienced a pickup in the pace of progress. Whether this faster pace of progress persists, or subsides once these smaller companies complete their climb up to the next plateau, remains an important question.

equal the supernormal return earned by computers. Then, based on the same logic as applied in equation 2-1, a shift from point A to point B in figure 2-2 would boost the nation's output by:

(2-5)   The boost to output with supernormal returns

$$= r_{SUPER} (K_2 - K_1).$$

To the extent that r_{SUPER} exceeds r_{COMP}, computers would boost output more than indicated by the basic neoclassical framework. Chapter 4 will consider various estimates of the plausible magnitude of supernormal returns.

Welfare Effects: Net Output

Although the growth-accounting framework described above is very useful for understanding how inputs are translated into output, it misses important features of the aggregate impact of computers on economic well-being, or what economists call economic welfare.[15]

The contribution of computing services to net output—that is, output net of depreciation—provides a more appropriate gauge of the welfare effects of the rising stock of computer equipment than does the contribution to gross, or total, output.[16] To see this point concretely, consider an extreme example. Suppose a machine were invented that could produce $7 trillion of output each year, doubling the size of the U.S. economy. Suppose further, however, that this machine depreciated fully in a year and cost $7 trillion to replace. On a gross basis, the machine would make a massive contribution to growth and would have a large impact on the structure of production. However, from a welfare point of view, the machine would be useless. All the income generated by the machine would be needed for its replacement, leaving none to support consumption spending. Thus, the machine's contribution to economic welfare, or well-being, would be zero.

15. This section draws heavily from Oliner and Sichel (1994), including text that is taken directly from pp. 286–88.

16. Over the years, there has been a heated debate between Edward Denison and Dale Jorgenson about whether growth accounting should be done on a gross or net basis. See the collection of articles by Denison, Griliches, and Jorgenson in *Survey of Current Business*, vol. 52 (May 1972). More recently, Hulten (1992, p. 9) argued that Denison and Jorgenson were both right. The two methods of growth accounting "are not substitutes, but complements which reveal different aspects of the growth process: gross product is the correct output concept for estimating the structure of production, while net product is the correct concept for measuring the welfare consequences of economic growth."

Equation 2-2 showed that the neoclassical contribution of computers to output growth equaled an income share, s_C, multiplied by the growth rate of the computer capital stock. As equations 2-3 and 2-4 showed, this income share is built up from a gross return, $r_{COMP} + d$, that includes a term for depreciation. By dropping the term for depreciation, an income share net of depreciation can be calculated as can the contribution of computers to output growth net of depreciation. Recall from above that two-thirds of the neoclassical gross rate of return to computers is accounted for by the costs of deprecation and obsolescence. Thus, netting out depreciation can be expected to reduce substantially the contribution of computers to output growth, as will be seen in chapter 4, where estimates of net contributions are presented.

Welfare Effects: Consumer Surplus

The estimates described thus far capture the impact of computing services on measures of income or output. Besides the output kick, however, there is a further benefit to society from declining computer prices that is not captured by those estimates. Return to figure 2-2 and again consider the shift from Supply 1 to Supply 2. Even at point A before prices fell, many computers were already purchased each year. As the price of computers declines from P_1 to P_2, those who were already buying computers at P_1 receive a bonus because they need no longer pay that higher price. Economists refer to this bonus as consumer surplus. As the price falls from P_1 to P_2, these extra benefits—each decrement in price times the number of computers previously purchased—trace out the area under the demand curve between the two prices; that is, the region marked off by P_1P_2BA.[17]

Although the simple story in figure 2-2 suggests that those who purchase computers receive the consumer surplus, this may not always be the case for computers. Because many computers are purchased by businesses to produce other goods or services, the consumer surplus may flow

17. Estimates of consumer surplus are discussed in chapter 4. Strictly speaking, the demand curve used to measure consumer surplus should be a compensated demand curve rather than the regular demand curves shown in figures 2-1 and 2-2. Because of the decline in computer prices, consumers' real incomes are larger, and some of this additional income may induce additional purchases of computers; that is, there may be an income effect. A compensated demand curve would remove these income effects. Provided income effects are small, however, the area under a standard demand curve should be a reasonable approximation to true consumer surplus. See Willig (1976).

downstream under certain circumstances. For example, consider a retailer that installs a computer-based inventory management system to lower costs. If this retailer could continue charging the same price for merchandise, the retailer's markup would rise because expenses would be lower. But, if every other retailer in the same market installed the same inventory-management system, then competitive pressures likely would push prices down. Depending on how this process worked out, the retailers' customers could receive much of the benefit of the new inventory systems.

The Productivity Paradox

In the past decade, vigorous debates have taken place in academic circles and in the broader media about the role of computers in economic growth.[18] The analytic framework presented above can provide some useful perspective on these debates. More generally, plausible ranges of computers' contribution to economic growth can be established under a variety of scenarios, by plugging in numerical estimates for the pieces of the growth accounting equation. As discussed in chapter 4, this exercise places limits on the contribution of computers to aggregate economic growth.

One specific aspect of these debates has been the question of why the economy's productivity performance has been lackluster at the same time as an explosion has occurred in computing power, the so-called productivity paradox. Early on, this debate was fueled by some academic research finding that computers earned a subpar return, leading some observers to suggest that companies might be earning less than a competitive return on these high-technology investments.[19] As for the broader paradox about aggregate productivity growth, economic historian Paul David summarized the paradox as follows:

> Disappointments with 'the computer revolution' and the newly dawned 'information age' in this regard have been keenly felt.

18. For excellent reviews of this literature, see National Research Council (1994); Brynjolfsson (1993); and Wilson (1993). For less academic versions of the debate, see Peter de Jager and J. Yannis Bakos, "Are Computers Boosting Productivity?" *ComputerWorld*, March 27, 1995, pp. 128–30; and Kristin Leutwyler, "Productivity Lost: Have Computers Meant Less Efficiency?" *Scientific American*, November 1994, pp. 101–02.

19. For example, see Osterman (1986); Loveman (1994); and Morrison and Berndt (1991).

Indeed, the notion that there is something anomalous about the prevailing state of affairs has drawn much of its appeal from the apparent failure of the wave of innovations based on the microprocessor and the memory chip to elicit a surge of growth in productivity from the sectors of the U.S. economy that recently have been investing so heavily in electronic data processing equipment.[20]

And Nobel-Prize-winning economist Robert Solow summed up the productivity paradox with the quip, "You can see the computer age everywhere but in the productivity statistics."[21]

Although an academic consensus has not emerged about how computers have affected economic growth, much important research has been completed and several interesting explanations of the computer paradox have been put forward. Each of these explanations tends to focus on an aspect of the linkages between computers and economic growth, including the rate of return earned by computers and the share of computers in the capital stock. Because the analytic framework presented here explicitly highlights these linkages, it provides a useful perspective on different explanations of the computer paradox.

Explanations of the computer paradox have been reviewed by other authors and are described only briefly here. These explanations fall into six broad categories: mismanagement, redistribution, long learning lags, mismeasurement, offsetting factors, and the small share of computers in the capital stock.[22] The first four focus on the rate of return earned by computers, while the last two emphasize broader aspects of computers' role in the economy.

The *mismanagement hypothesis* suggests that companies may underestimate the full costs of information technology and therefore misallocate their information technology resources. In terms of figure 2-2, this explanation posits that firms underestimate the true price of their computer resources and move too far down the demand curve. By moving below the true price on the demand curve, firms overinvest in computer resources and earn less than a competitive (or neoclassical) return on their computer investments.

20. David (1990, p. 355).

21. Robert M. Solow, "We'd Better Watch Out," *New York Times Book Review*, July 12, 1987, p. 36.

22. For example, see Baily and Gordon (1988); Brynjolfsson (1993); National Research Council (1994); and Oliner and Sichel (1994). The discussion of the mismanagement, redistribution, long learning lags, and mismeasurement hypotheses draws heavily from Brynjolfsson, pp. 11–19.

For example, managers might underestimate the total cost of purchasing, operating, and supporting desktop computers. According to one consulting firm, "costs associated with the PC remain 'subtle, hidden and excessive.'" This report found that large companies spend $3,830 every year to maintain each personal computer. Helpdesk support and downtime accounted for the biggest chunks.[23] Downtime can also be very expensive. According to a Gallup survey of the top 1,000 firms in the country, the "average corporate LAN [local area network] goes down 27 times a year, costing its owner nearly $3.5 million in lost productivity and about $600,000 in vaporized revenue."[24] Similarly, employees may spend significant time learning how to use their computers. Another consulting firm reported that "business PC users waste 5.1 hours each week 'futzing' with their computers—learning how to use them, waiting for them to do things, checking the things they do, and so on."[25] Overall, this consulting firm estimated that "futzing" costs business nearly $100 billion a year. Anecdotes such as these must be taken with a large grain of salt. Nevertheless, if managers do not correctly assess all of these costs, companies could well earn less than a competitive return on their computer investments.

The *redistribution hypothesis* also focuses on rates of return, in particular on possible differences between private and social rates of return. This explanation conjectures that many computers are deployed for tasks that generate substantial private value by redistributing wealth from one person to another but do little to boost overall productivity. For example, traders on Wall Street rely heavily on sophisticated information technology to identify profitable trades faster than competitors. These traders stand to gain a lot if they are the first to identify these opportunities, making it well worth investing in the latest and best technology. Thus, even if firms in this business make rational decisions about computer purchases, the impact of this equipment on the overall output of the financial services industry might be small because the computers are primarily being used to redistribute profits among traders rather than to

23. Report by Forrester Research, Inc., as reported in the *Wall Street Journal*, February 16, 1995, p. A1.
24. As reported in Becky J. Campbell, "Network Snooze," *CompuServe Magazine*, December 1994, pp. 24–30, especially p. 24.
25. Report by Software Business Technology (SBT), Inc., as reported in James Krohe Jr., "The Productivity Pit," *Across the Board*, October 1993, pp. 16–21, especially p. 18.

generate greater output of financial services. Put in the language of economics, this hypothesis conjectures that computers generate a healthy private return—inducing large investments in computers—but a smaller social return. If computers are used extensively for redistribution activities, the measured return on this equipment to the financial services industry or the economy as a whole could be subpar.[26]

The *long learning-lags hypothesis* conjectures that information technology ultimately will generate a large productivity payoff but that it takes a long time for companies to learn how to use this equipment effectively and to begin earning higher rates of return. Paul David has put this hypothesis forward most forcefully.[27] He suggests that new technologies diffuse slowly, and he makes a historical analogy to electric motors. Most of the technical developments required for commercial application of electricity occurred before 1880, but it was not until the 1920s that the productivity benefits were reaped. If this analogy applies to computers, then big payoffs will begin to emerge in the future as companies learn how to exploit fully the capabilities of new computer technologies. But, because the payoffs from computers would be realized long after the investments were made, a comparison of current costs to current benefits could give the appearance of subpar returns, even though firms would eventually earn competitive or better rates of return on these investments.

The *mismeasurement hypothesis* conjectures that computing equipment actually generates a competitive or better return but that the current system of national accounts misses benefits of computers that are notoriously difficult to measure including quality, variety, and convenience.[28] To the extent that benefits of computers are not measured, the measured rates of return for computers would be less than the actual return, giving the false impression that computers earn less than a competitive return.

The *offsetting factors hypothesis* posits that computers have made a substantial contribution to economic growth in recent decades but that other factors have dragged down economic growth sufficiently to make overall growth appear sluggish.

The *small share of computers in the capital stock hypothesis* notes that

26. In an interesting discussion of the output of stock exchanges and information, Bresnahan, Milgrom, and Paul (1992) suggest that substantial gaps are likely between private and social incentives in stock trading.

27. David (1989, 1990).

28. See Baily and Gordon (1988); and Griliches (1994).

computers make up a relatively small share of the overall capital stock. According to this view, if computers earn a competitive rate of return in individual applications, their contribution to overall economic growth would be limited by their modest size relative to all other capital.

Establishing the relative importance of these hypotheses is well beyond the scope of this book, requiring precise estimates of private and social rates of return earned by computers. Estimating such returns in a way that would be incontrovertible is a tall order.[29] Nevertheless, the empirical implementation of this analytic framework in chapter 4 will highlight important aspects of computers' role in economic growth and will shed light on several of the proposed explanations of the computer paradox.

Appendix: The Contribution of Computers to Output Growth

Equation 2-1 showed that the increment to income of an increase in the stock of computers equals the return earned by computers multiplied by the change in the stock of computers. Namely,

$$(2A\text{-}1) \qquad (Y_2 - Y_1)_C = r_{COMP} (K_2 - K_1).$$

where $(Y_2 - Y_1)_C$ is the increment to income generated by computers. Let the income increment on the left-hand side and the change in the capital stock on the right-hand side represent changes from one year to the next. The subscript c on the left-hand side indicates that this equation just captures the increment to income from an increase in the stock of computers and not from any other factors that might boost income.

Equation 2A-1 has not distinguished between real and nominal income. If Y and K represent real quantities, then we must insert a term that takes account of differences in the relative prices associated with Y and K. Specifically, insert P_c/P into the right-hand side of equation (2A-1), where P_c is the price index for computers and P is the price index for output. This yields:

$$(Y_2 - Y_1)_C = [r_{COMP} (P_C/P)] (K_2 - K_1).$$

29. Box 4-2 discusses evidence from the focused interviews confirming the difficulties faced by companies in measuring the benefits from information technology, even though these companies have access to proprietary data that would not be available to most researchers.

Next, note that in equation 2A-1, r_{COMP} is the rate of return net of depreciation. The total increment to income would include the income flow that goes to cover depreciation. Let the rate of depreciation equal d. Then, the rate of return covering depreciation would equal $(r_{COMP} + d)$, leading to:

$$(2A-3) \qquad (Y_2 - Y_1)_C = [(r_{COMP} + d) (P_C/P)](K_2 - K_1).$$

Equation 2A-3 shows the increment to real output from an increase in the stock of computers between year 1 and year 2. To convert this to growth rates, divide both sides by Y_1 and multiply and divide the right-hand side by K_1, yielding

$$(2A-4) \qquad (Y_2 - Y_1)_C/Y_1 = [(r_{COMP} + d) (P_C/P) (K_1/Y_1)]$$
$$[(K_2 - K_1)/K_1].$$

Now, for simplicity of exposition, replace $(Y_2 - Y_1)_c/Y_1$ and $(K_2 - K_1)/K_1$ with $\dot{Y}_c$ and $\dot{K}_c$, respectively, where these terms represent the contribution of computers to real output growth and the growth rate of the real stock of computers. This substitution yields

$$(2A-5) \qquad \dot{Y}_C = [(r_{COMP} + d) (P_c/P) (K_1/Y_1)] \dot{K}_c.$$

Next, to make the notation more general, replace (K_1/Y_1) with (K_c/Y), where K_c is the real stock of computers and Y is total real output in a given year. This last substitution yields

$$(2A-6) \qquad \dot{Y}_c = [(r_{COMP} + d) (P_c/P) (K_c/Y)] \dot{K}_c.$$

Equation 2A-6 shows the contribution of computers to output growth.

To see that the terms in square brackets in equation 2A-6 represent the nominal income share of computers, rearrange terms as

$$(2A-7) \qquad \dot{Y}_c = [\{(r_{COMP} + d) P_c K_c\} / PY] \dot{K}_c.$$

The term that in braces equals the nominal stock of computers, $P_c K_c$, multiplied by the rate of return earned by computers, $(r_{comp} + d)$; this product yields the total income flow generated by the stock of computers.

Once the term in braces is divided by total income *PY*, the result is the share of income generated by computers. Designating this income share as s_C yields:

(2A-8)
$$\dot{Y}_c = s_c \dot{K}_c$$

which is the same as equation 2-2 in the text.

CHAPTER 3

Computer Hardware and Software in the Economy

T O UNDERSTAND the role of computers in the economy, and to implement the framework described in the last chapter, the basic facts about the use of computer hardware and software in the economy must be understood. For the reasons described in chapter 1, this review focuses on computer hardware and software used in the business sector.

Computer hardware is a surprisingly small share of the total capital stock. Hardware, however, is never used in isolation. Rather, it must be combined with software for anything of value to be done. For office-based users of information technology, tasks accomplished with a computer are almost always associated with specific software applications. In most office settings, word processors and spreadsheets used on a personal computer (PC) are typically the most extensively used applications.[1] In many lines of business, specialized PC applications are important, too. For example, some engineering firms rely heavily on computer-aided design (CAD) software to automate development and production of engineering drawings, while some law firms rely on software tools that allow rapid search of legal databases. In addition, software that allows users in different physical locations to work collaboratively across a network—such as Lotus Notes—is a relatively new entry that has received much attention. On mainframe systems, complex software applications allow financial services companies to handle a tremendous transactions volume, while retailers can track sales and inventories of an immense number of products.[2]

As these examples make clear, software should be included when assessing the impact of computers, although lack of data has made it difficult to include software in a comprehensive way. Using what data

1. See table 3-5.
2. Examples are drawn from the interviews.

are available, later sections in this chapter provide a rough look at software sales and prices in recent years, highlighting the important role played by software.

In this chapter, data on quantities and prices of software are used to assess how measurement of the nation's gross domestic product (GDP) might change if software's coverage were expanded to treat software more like hardware in the National Income Accounts. In the GDP accounts to date, software's coverage has been limited; much software purchased by businesses is not included as an investment good (capitalized asset), in contrast to computer hardware and other physical capital. Rough estimates suggest that broader coverage of software would noticeably boost the level and growth rates of business investment in the accounts. As for real GDP, broader coverage of software might boost the level of real GDP by as much as three-quarters of a percent, but would have a very limited impact on its growth rate because software's share in GDP is just too small to have much impact on overall GDP growth rates.

Computer Hardware in the Economy

The Commerce Department's Bureau of Economic Analysis (BEA) publishes data that provide a useful overview of computer hardware. In particular, their series for investment in computer and peripheral equipment (CPE) measures business purchases of PCs, workstations, minicomputers, mainframes, client-server systems, and the peripherals—such as printers and communications links—used with these computers.[3] This series provides a natural starting point for collecting some basic facts about hardware; CPE, along with its associated capital stock series, is described in more detail in the Appendix to this chapter.

Computer Hardware Intensity in the Overall Economy

To gauge the intensity of computer use in the economy, it is useful to look at investment and capital stock shares of computers. For selected

3. Analysts often have used the broader category office, computing, and accounting machinery (OCA), but the constant-dollar version of this series suffers from the index number problems discussed in the Appendix to this chapter. These problems arise because OCA includes computers and old-fashioned office equipment like typewriters, whose prices have not fallen as fast as computer prices. The constant-dollar OCA series does not take account of these relative price changes, leading to biased measures of growth in the series.

Table 3-1. *Computers and Peripheral Equipment as a Share of Total Nonresidential Equipment and Structures*

Percent

Item	1970	1975	1980	1985	1990	1993
Real share[a]						
Investment	0.1	0.2	1.0	4.7	8.7	17.8
Net capital stock	0.0	0.1	0.2	1.2	2.8	4.7
Nominal share						
Investment	2.6	2.1	3.5	6.4	6.3	7.6
Net capital stock	.9	.6	.9	1.8	2.0	1.8
Addendum						
Nominal share, net capital stock						
Office, computing, and						
accounting equipment	1.7	1.4	1.6	2.1	2.3	2.0
Information processing equipment	7.5	7.5	8.0	10.5	11.4	11.6

Source: Based on Oliner and Sichel (1994), using data from U.S. Department of Commerce, Bureau of Economic Analysis. Numbers for the real and nominal net capital stock of computers and peripheral equipment differ slightly from Oliner and Sichel, reflecting the correction of a minor programming error.

a. Real series are in 1987 dollars. As discussed in the text and Appendix to chapter 3, these real shares are biased because of index number problems and must be interpreted with caution.

years, the top panel of table 3-1 shows shares of CPE as a fraction of all nonresidential equipment and structures. As the first line shows, CPE has accounted for a rapidly rising share of real investment, increasing from less than 1 percent before 1980 to almost 18 percent in 1993. Similarly, the share of CPE out of the real capital stock also has surged, although the capital stock share is notably lower than the investment share.

As Stephen D. Oliner and Daniel E. Sichel point out, however, these real shares—although often cited—have little meaning and can be made to take on almost any value depending on the base year chosen.[4] As described in more detail in the Appendix to this chapter, rebasing real computer investment to 1992 dollars instead of 1987 dollars, leads to a much lower real CPE share because computers would now be valued at lower 1992 prices. And a base year can be chosen to yield almost any real share.

In contrast, nominal shares are unaffected by choice of base year. Quite sensibly, the nominal share reveals the share of the capital stock in each year *evaluated in the prices actually faced by purchasers and producers in that year.*[5] As can be seen in figure 3-1 (and table 3-1), the

4. Oliner and Sichel (1994, p. 278).

5. As explained in the Appendix, real, or constant-dollar, values of the computer capital

Figure 3-1. *Share of Computers in Total Nonresidential Net Capital Stock (current dollars)*

Percent

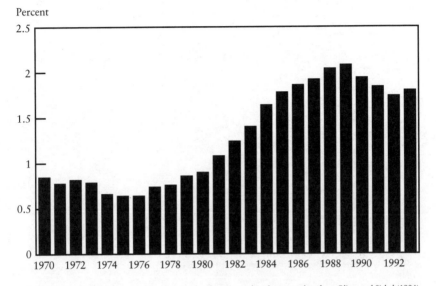

Source: Nominal net stock for computers and peripheral equipment based on procedure from Oliner and Sichel (1994), using U.S. Department of Commerce, Bureau of Economic Analysis investment data and weights. Total nominal stock from BEA. Differs slightly from Oliner and Sichel, reflecting correction of a minor programming error.

nominal CPE capital-stock share was fairly stable in the 1970s and then increased notably during the 1980s. In the early 1990s, this share dropped back a little, as the recession pulled down the stock of computer capital more than other capital. By 1993 CPE accounted for less than 2 percent of the net capital stock. Thus computers remain a relatively small input to production.

Often, observers find this small capital stock share puzzling; how can computers make up such a tiny share of the capital stock if companies spend billions of dollars on computers every year? A key reason is that computers become obsolete so rapidly. Much new spending on computers goes to replacing and updating older equipment. For example, the Commerce Department estimates that during the 1980s more than half of the new investment in computers and office equipment was required just to keep up with depreciation, even after taking account of the improvements in the capabilities of computers during the decade.[6] Put an-

stock are appropriate for certain purposes, such as the growth rates shown in figures 1-1 and 1-2.

6. Constant-dollar depreciation and investment figures for OCA are taken from U.S. Department of Commerce (1993, pp. 169, 375).

other way, while computers are coming in the front door at a good clip, they also are going out the back door at a hefty pace.

For completeness, the addendum in table 3-1 also shows the nominal capital stock shares for the broader categories of office, computing, and accounting equipment (OCA), and information-processing equipment. In recent years when CPE has accounted for most of OCA, the OCA and CPE capital stock shares are little different. In earlier years, the OCA share is higher. In contrast, the nominal capital stock share of information-processing equipment is quite a bit larger, reaching 11.7 percent by 1993. For the most part, the higher share reflects a large stock of communication equipment. As indicated earlier, however, this broader category is not the primary focus of this study.

Computer Hardware Intensity across Industries

Because data for CPE are not available on an industry basis, comparisons across industries must rely on a broader measure.[7] The narrowest measure available across industries is the OCA category described earlier.[8] Table 3-2 shows the distribution of the nominal net stock of office equipment (OCA) across industries for selected years from 1950 to 1993. As the table reveals, more than three-fourths of the nation's stock of OCA was used by service-producing industries in 1993. Among service-producing industries, finance, insurance, and real estate is the heaviest user of this office equipment, accounting for more than a third of the total stock. Finally, note that the service-sector share has picked up appreciably over time. Back in 1950—well before the widespread use of electronic computers—the service sector used less than half of the nominal OCA stock.

Viewed from this perspective, computers appear to have a disproportionately large effect on the service sector. Although the service sector is more computer-intensive than the goods sector, the extent to which this is true can be easily overstated. Just as the service sector uses a large share of the computers in the economy, the service sector also produces a large share of the output in the economy and uses a large share of the total capital stock. For example, in 1992 the service-producing sector accounted for almost 72 percent of the economy's output and almost 70 percent of the total nonresidential private capital stock, in nominal terms.

7. Stiroh (1996) includes a similar analysis of computer use across industries.
8. Nominal OCA—used to compute these nominal shares—does not suffer from the index-number problems that afflict constant-dollar OCA.

Table 3-2. *Industry Distribution of Nominal Net Stock of Office, Computing, and Accounting Equipment (OCA), 1950–93*

Share of OCA stock in each industry, percent

Industry	1950	1960	1970	1980	1990	1993
All industries	100.0	100.0	100.0	100.0	100.0	100.0
Goods-producing industries	50.4	39.3	36.2	33.4	23.1	22.7
Agriculture, forestry, and fisheries	0.0	0.0	0.2	0.1	0.1	0.1
Mining	0.4	1.2	0.9	2.5	1.3	0.8
Construction	1.8	1.9	1.2	0.3	0.3	0.2
Manufacturing	48.2	36.2	33.9	30.4	21.4	21.6
Service-producing industries	49.6	60.7	63.8	66.7	76.9	77.3
Transportation and public utilities	17.3	13.0	7.1	4.3	6.5	6.5
Wholesale trade	6.3	6.2	10.1	12.3	11.2	11.9
Retail trade	3.7	3.9	4.0	3.2	5.5	7.8
Finance, insurance, and real estate	15.9	23.0	26.5	34.1	36.6	34.6
Services	6.4	14.8	16.1	12.7	17.2	16.6

Source: Unpublished data from U.S. Department of Commerce, Bureau of Economic Analysis.

Table 3-3 makes the same point another way. This table shows the share of OCA within the capital stock of each industry; for each industry, these numbers are the rough analog of the computer intensity figures shown in table 3-1. This share varies considerably across industries from a high of 5.2 percent in wholesale trade in 1993 to a low of 0.1 percent in agriculture. But a look at broader sectors of the economy shows this share differed more modestly between goods and service-producing sectors in 1993, equaling 1.5 percent for goods and 2.2 percent for services.

Software Sales and Employment

Data from several sources demonstrate the rapid growth of sales and employment in the software industry. These basic figures also demonstrate that purchases of software are nearly as large as those of hardware, even when a narrow definition of software is used.

Table 3-3. *Computer Intensity by Industry, 1950–93*

Percent

Industry[a]	1950	1960	1970	1980	1990	1993
All industries	1.0	1.4	1.6	1.5	2.2	2.0
Goods-producing industries	1.3	1.4	1.5	1.3	1.6	1.5
Agriculture, forestry, and fisheries	0.0	0.0	0.0	0.0	0.1	0.1
Mining	0.1	0.3	0.3	0.5	0.6	0.5
Construction	0.9	1.5	1.0	0.2	0.5	0.4
Manufacturing	2.2	2.2	2.3	2.0	2.2	2.0
Service-producing industries	0.8	1.3	1.6	1.6	2.5	2.2
Transportation and public utilities	0.4	0.5	0.4	0.2	0.6	0.6
Wholesale trade	3.1	4.3	5.4	5.5	5.4	5.2
Retail trade	0.7	1.1	1.2	0.9	1.8	2.1
Finance, insurance, and real estate	1.4	2.5	2.5	3.0	3.4	2.9
Services	1.5	3.5	3.3	2.5	4.1	3.5

Source: Unpublished data from U.S. Department of Commerce, Bureau of Economic Analysis.

a. For each industry, the nominal share of net capital stock of office computers and accounting equipment in total capital, percent.

Aggregate Software Sales

Montgomery Phister was one of the first to assemble data on revenues of the software industry, providing estimates from 1963 to 1974 for mainframe systems, which Phister indicates accounted for the bulk of software at that time.[9] As described by Phister, an independent software industry was just getting started in this period. It was writing assemblers, compilers, and utility routines for hardware manufacturers and application programs for users. According to Phister's estimates, revenues in this fledgling industry rose very rapidly from virtually zero in the early 1960s to about $1 billion in 1974, as shown in figure 3-2 and table 3-4.

This $1 billion figure, however, only captures a narrow definition of software expenses. It only covers purchases of software from independent software companies. As Phister reports, this segment accounted for a small share of total software expenses in 1974. Development costs incurred by hardware manufacturers accounted for another small slice, coming to $300 million in 1974. The bulk of expenses, however, was accounted for by costs incurred by users to write and maintain software in house, amounting to almost $9 billion in 1974.[10] Total software expenses came to about $10 billion in 1974.

9. Phister (1979, pp. 24–27).
10. Phister (1979, pp. 25, 27, figures 1.25.1, 1.25.2, 1.25.4).

Figure 3-2. *Software Industry Revenues, 1963–74[a]*

Billions of dollars

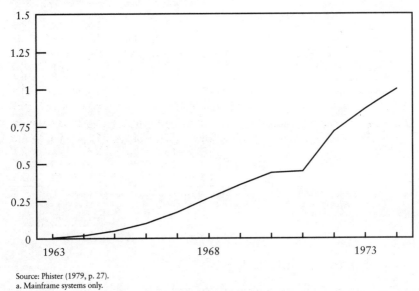

Source: Phister (1979, p. 27).
a. Mainframe systems only.

Phister's range of estimates highlights two important points. First, development costs by in-house users are a substantial portion of total software costs, although some of this reflects maintenance costs rather than development of new programs or capabilities. More recently, as the software industry has matured and easy-to-use applications have become widely available, the share of in-house costs appears to have fallen.[11] Nevertheless, even with the widespread use of shrink-wrapped PC software today, many users still spend much time customizing and developing specialized software applications.

11. Zraket (1992, p. 291) cites estimates of software output in 1988, which use a broad definition that includes in-house development of software. These estimates imply that including software developed by hardware manufacturers and by users in house roughly doubles the size of the software industry. Although a factor of two is significant, it is much less than Phister's estimate that including these additional categories of software costs boosted software expenses by a factor of ten in 1974. Zraket's figures also indicate that the Defense Department is a heavy consumer of software. Unfortunately, Zraket's figures only provide a snapshot of one year, providing little information about how software expenses have changed over time. OECD (1994, p. 27) provides additional support for the ratio found by Zraket. This report indicates that total software spending in the United States is about double the spending on packaged software.

Table 3-4. *Revenues of U.S. Software Industry, 1963–93, and Average Annual Growth Rates, 1984–93*

Billions of dollars unless otherwise indicated

Revenue, Phister's data		Revenue, U.S. Bureau of the Census data			
		Including integrated compuer systems[a]		Excluding integrated computer systems[b]	
Year	Sales	Year	Sales	Year	Sales
1963	$0.01	1984	$19.1	...	...
1964	0.02	1985	21.0	...	...
1965	0.05	1986	24.0	...	...
1966	0.10	1987	28.1	...	...
1967	0.18	1988	34.8	...	...
1968	0.27	1989	40.5	...	...
1969	0.36	1990 (old)	43.7	...	...
1970	0.44				
1971	0.45	1990 (new)	49.8	1990 (new)	31.2
1972	0.72	1991	54.1	1991	34.3
1973	0.87	1992	59.5	1992	37.6
1974	1.00	1993	67.4	1993	42.8

Addendum

Average annual growth rates (average log differences times 100)

Including integrated computer systems[a]
1984–90	13.8
1987–90	14.7
1990–93	10.1
1987–93[c]	12.4

Excluding integrated computer systems[b]
1987–93[d]	12.6
1990–93	10.5

Source: 1963–74 from Phister (1979, pp. 27, figure 1.25.3, p. 277). Figures from 1984 to 1990 on the old basis are from U.S. Department of Commerce, Bureau of the Census, *Current Business Reports: Service Annual Survey* (1990), table 1A. On the 1972 SIC classification, these figures correspond to industry 7372. Figures from 1990 to 1993 on the new basis are from Bureau of the Census, *Current Business Reports: Service Annual Survey* (1993), p. 20, table 4.1.

a. On the new 1987 SIC, industries 7371, 7372, and 7373.

b. On the new 1987 SIC, industries 7371 and 7372.

c. Total log difference calculated as the sum of the log difference from 1987 to 1990 (old basis) plus the log difference from 1990 (new basis) to 1993. This sum is divided by 6 to get the figure reported in the table.

d. Includes integrated systems from 1987 to 1990 and excludes them from 1990 to 1993. Total log difference calculated as the sum of the log difference from 1987 to 1990 for data including integrated systems plus the log difference from 1990 to 1993 for data excluding integrated systems. This sum is divided by 6 to get the figure reported in the table.

Second, software expenses can be defined narrowly or broadly. A focus just on the industry primarily engaged in designing and developing software leads to a narrow definition, while the inclusion of all software-related expenses incurred by any company or employee in the economy obviously yields a much broader definition. Ideally, it would be desirable

Figure 3-3. *Software Industry Revenues, 1963–93*

Billions of dollars

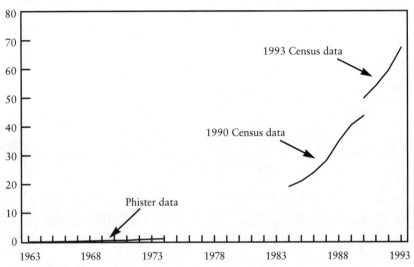

Source: Phister (1979); and U.S. Department of Commerce, Bureau of the Census, *Current Business Reports: Service Annual Survey* (1990, 1993).

to have reliable estimates over time for both the narrower and broader concepts. As a practical matter, however, developing reliable estimates of development costs incurred by users is virtually impossible. Moreover, there is no way to know what share of these expenses reflects development of new capabilities versus maintenance. Thus it will be necessary to rely largely on narrower definitions that focus primarily on the software industry.

For the software industry, Phister's estimates of sales can be extended with data from the Census Bureau, although there is a discontinuity until 1984. Beginning in that year, the Census Bureau began estimating receipts for the industry "computer programming and other software services."[12] Figure 3-3 and table 3-4 show these Census receipts for computer programming and other software services from 1984 to 1993,

12. This industry classification includes a bit more than just independent software producers. It covers the design and production of prepackaged software; custom programming done on a contract basis; and the design, sale, and installation of integrated computer systems. This last category does not strictly belong in the independent software industry, because an important part of that business consists of combining and reselling hardware items. Nevertheless, there is no alternative but to include it because further detail is not available between1984 and 1990.

along with Phister's data for the earlier period.[13] Although the measures in the figure and table are incomplete and do not provide exactly the right coverage, there can be no doubt that revenues in the software industry have surged ahead since the early 1960s. From 1984 to 1990, revenues in this industry more than doubled, implying an annual rate of growth of nearly 14 percent. Although definitional changes cause a discontinuity in the series in 1990, the extension of this series from 1990 to 1993 indicates that revenues increased at an annual rate of more than 10 percent. In part, the slowdown in growth reflects the recession 1990–91.

In 1990 the Census Bureau began reporting new industry definitions and collecting more detail for these industries, allowing a more accurate gauge of the size of the software industry.[14] In particular, the extra detail makes it possible to strip out establishments selling integrated computer systems and to include only receipts for the computer programming services and the prepackaged software industries. These data are also shown in table 3-4, rising at an annual rate exceeding 10 percent between 1990 and 1993.

These figures can be used to put the size and importance of software into perspective. Sales of the software industry—excluding integrated computer systems—were $42.8 billion in 1993.[15] By way of comparison, nominal spending for computer and peripheral equipment was $47.0 billion in 1993.[16] Thus, in terms of yearly purchases, software is almost

13. For data from 1984 to 1990, see U.S. Department of Commerce, Bureau of the Census, *Current Business Reports: Service Annual Survey* (1990), p.6. This industry was identified as SIC number 7372, according to the old 1972 Standard Industrial Classification numbers. Besides the *Service Annual Survey*, the Census Bureau does a quinquennial census of service industries, with the most recent one done in 1992. Ultimately, the figures in the annual survey will be benchmarked to the 1992 Census. For the later data, see *Current Business Reports: Service Annual Survey* (1993), p. 20, table 4-1.

14. In the 1987 SIC, the old industry 7372 was divided into computer programming services, prepackaged software, and computer integrated systems design, classified as 7371, 7372, and 7373, respectively. Besides the division of the broader category, some other definitional changes accompanied the 1987 SIC reclassification. See Executive Office of the President (1987, pp. 365–67, 676).

15. Bureau of the Census, *Current Business Reports: Service Annual Survey* (1993), p. 20, table 4-1. Besides the industry breakdown described in the text—in which all of an establishment's receipts are allocated to the industry in which it is primarily engaged—this survey also provides a breakdown of receipts by source. That is, for the much broader industry that includes data processing (SIC number 737), this breakdown allocates receipts within each firm by type of product sold. On this basis, firms within SIC industry number 737 sold $39.4 billion of computer programming and prepackaged software in 1993, as shown in *Service Annual Survey* (1993), p. 20.

16. U.S. Department of Commerce, *Survey of Current Business*, vol. 74 (July 1994), table 5-8, p. 84.

as important as hardware, even when a fairly narrow definition of software is used.

Sales by Type of Software

The aggregate data just described would be sufficient for assessing the productivity impact of software on the overall economy. Some data, however, are available at a finer level of detail, gathered by consulting firms and trade associations. For example, the consulting firm Digital Information Group, reports total software sales of $31.0 billion in 1992, which is not too much below the $37.6 billion Census Bureau figure for nominal sales of the software industry, excluding integrated computer systems. Of the total reported by the Digital Information Group, table 3-5 shows that almost half of all software sales in 1992 were purchases of disk-based microsoftware. Just over 40 percent of sales represented software for supercomputers, mainframes, and minicomputers. Interestingly, more than 10 percent of all software sales were accounted for by video game cartridges.[17]

Within microcomputer software, further detail is available, through the use of data from the Software Publishers Association (SPA) for sales in North America. These data cover PC applications software, excluding operating systems.[18] Not surprisingly, word processors are the most important application, followed by spreadsheets and database programs, as shown in the lower part of table 3-5. Perhaps somewhat surprisingly, these three applications accounted for just 34.3 percent of all sales of PC applications software in 1992, with entertainment applications next in line.[19]

Finally, the addendum in table 3-5 shows that from 1987 to 1993 nominal sales of PC Applications software increased at an annual average rate of 20 percent.[20] This pace is substantially faster than the 12 percent average annual growth in overall software revenue indicated by the figures in table

---

17. Figures for 1992 are reported in Digital Information Group (1993, table 1-2, p. 3).

18. Because Microsoft is such a big player in operating systems, any data put out by the SPA would essentially amount to releasing proprietary data about Microsoft; therefore, the SPA does not release figures for operating systems. The SPA is the Washington-based trade association for publishers of microcomputer software. See SPA's press releases on software sales.

19. Ranking is based on sales figures for 1993 from the SPA.

20. The detailed data from the SPA, showing annual sales of PC applications software from 1987 to 1993 are shown in Appendix table 3A-1.

Table 3-5. *Software Sales of U.S. Companies by Type, 1992*[a]

Billions of dollars and percent shares

Item	Sales ($)	Share (%)
All software	31.0	100.0
Microsoftware (disk-based)	14.5	46.8
Mainframe, supercomputer, and minicomputer	13.2	42.6
Videogame cartridges	3.3	10.6
PC Applications software, North American sales[b,c]	5.7	100.0
Word processors	0.8	14.4
Spreadsheets	0.8	13.8
Database	0.3	6.1
Addendum		
Average growth of PC Applications software, 1987-93[d]		20.1

Source: Digital Information Group, *Software Indusry Factbook* (Stanford, Conn., 1993), table 1-2, p. 3. Detail on PC Applications software from the Software Publishers Association, Washington, DC.

a. Data are not comparable to those in table 3-4; these data are from a different source and cover a different definition of software.

b. The figure for sales of PC Applications is well below the estimate in the second line of the table for microsoftware. Microsoftware also includes operating systems and networking software, which are excluded from the Applications category.

c. Software shares calculated with original, nonrounded figures.

d. Based on data in Appendix table 3A-1; average log difference times 100.

3-4. This relationship is not surprising given the rapid shift in this period toward PCs and away from mainframes and minicomputers.

Employment in the Software Industry

Besides sales, employment provides another measure for gauging the size and growth of the software industry. Employment in the software industry has grown rapidly as well in the last decade, as shown in table 3-6. Actually calculating the rate of growth of computer-services labor is simple in principle, but serious measurement problems arise here as well. Difficulties arise because much computer-services labor represents work done by end users, rather than by employees of the software industry. Despite these difficulties, employment data from the Bureau of Labor Statistics can be used for a broader category than just software to get a rough idea of the pace of employment growth. This broader industry is computer and data processing; besides the three software industries described earlier, this broader industry includes all data processing, information retrieval services, and computer facilities management services. From 1984 to 1993, employment in the computer and data processing industry grew at a hefty 7 percent annual rate, well above the one and three-fourths percent growth in total nonagricultural employment over

Table 3-6. *Employment in the Computer and Data Processing Industry,*
1984–93

Year	Employment (thousands)	Growth rate[a] (percent)
1984	474.5	...
1985	541.6	13.3
1986	588.2	8.2
1987	628.8	6.7
1988	673.4	6.8
1989	736.3	8.9
1990	771.9	4.7
1991	797.1	3.2
1992	835.6	4.7
1993	902.9	7.7
Average annual growth rates[a]		
1984–93	...	7.1
1988–93	...	6.0

Source: Author's calculations based on U.S. Department of Labor, Bureau of Labor Statistics, *Employment and Earnings* (Washington, various issues). Employment from the establishment survey; covers computer programming and software and data processing services.
a. Log differences times 100.

this period.[21] Although this series is too broad (by including more than just the software industry) and too narrow (by excluding work done by end users), it confirms the rapid expansion of software and related industries.[22]

Software Prices

As shown in figure 1-3, the price of computer hardware has fallen dramatically in recent decades.[23] Recall that the price measure in that figure shows prices declining at an annual pace of 15.1 percent from 1970 to 1994, after accounting for each year's improvements in the quality of computer hardware. But what about prices of software?

21. U.S. Bureau of Labor Statistics, *Employment and Earnings*, establishment survey data from various issues.
22. Outsourcing could also lead to difficulties in interpreting these data. As outsourcing spreads and more companies purchase computer services from outside vendors, employment counted in the computer and data processing industry would be boosted by the shift of employees from computer-using industries, even if the employees did the same job in both industries.
23. Parts of this section are taken directly from Oliner and Sichel (1994).

Historically, software has been a craft industry, in which highly skilled professionals write code line by line. In the 1960s and 1970s several studies examined costs per line of software code written. Phister adopted an estimate of a 3.5 percent annual reduction in the labor required to produce one thousand lines of code.[24] Vijay C. Gurbaxani, taking account of Phister's estimate and others in the literature, used a 5 percent decline in the annual real cost of software development; that is, each year a given amount of software could be written for a cost 5 percent less than in the prior year, on an inflation-adjusted basis.[25] Charles Zraket argues that the nominal cost per line of code in the early 1990s was little changed from twenty years earlier, which would yield a real decline similar to Gurbaxani's.[26]

These estimates of a relatively slow pace of price decline for software—at least compared with hardware—are not really surprising. Hardware prices have plunged as semiconductor technology has leaped forward, but there is no analogous technological driver of price decline for software.[27] However, the evidence described above does not take account of the development of a mass market for prepackaged PC software. The development of a mass market could have important implications for pricing, because if the fixed costs of producing a software application can be spread over more customers, a lower unit price will be sufficient to recover these fixed costs.

To get at these issues, three recent studies have focused on prices of prepackaged PC software. Erik Brynjolfsson and Chris Kemerer as well as Neil Gandal estimated price indexes for spreadsheets.[28] Oliner and Sichel developed another price index for spreadsheets as well as indexes for word processors and database programs.[29] Before these studies are discussed, the techniques used by these authors to estimate price changes are briefly described.

---

24. Phister (1979, p. 502).

25. Gurbaxani (1990, chap. 2).

26. Zraket (1992) cites evidence that software for routine applications costs about $10 a line, while code for extremely demanding applications (like the space shuttle) might cost as much as $1,000 a line of debugged code. Zraket notes that these nominal costs have changed little during the prior two decades.

27. CASE tools (computer-aided software engineering tools) are one exception, but it is difficult to see how these tools could push down software prices as fast as improvements in semiconductors have driven down the price of hardware.

28. Brynjolfsson and Kemerer (1993); and Gandal (1994).

29. Oliner and Sichel (1994).

Matched Model and "Hedonic" Price Indexes

If product price data are available, estimating the change in average prices of products is completely straightforward; a good price index, however, must also adjust for changes in quality. For example, an early version of WordPerfect was advertised for $277 in mid-1984, while WordPerfect Version 6.0 for Windows could be purchased for about $276 in late 1993.[30] Would it make any sense to say that the nominal price of WordPerfect had not changed over this period, without taking account of the improvements in quality and functionality that make the later version of WordPerfect a different product than the first version? Obviously not, which leads to the difficulty of adjusting for quality change.

The studies looking at PC software prices have used two different techniques to adjust prices for quality change. The first, referred to as the "hedonic" technique, measures quality directly by identifying and quantifying specific features of products and assessing how these features change over time. For example, the Bureau of Economic Analysis uses a hedonic index for computer hardware, in which processor speed and memory size are the two most important controls for quality. Quality-adjusted price changes reflect changes in actual prices less the adjustment for quality changes.[31] For hardware, it is fairly clear that processor speed and memory capture the most important features generating value in the marketplace. But for complex and hard-to-describe products like software, identification of such characteristics is more problematic.

The second technique for quality adjustment uses "matched-models" to construct a price index.[32] In contrast to hedonic indexes that directly control for quality changes, matched-model indexes control for quality indirectly, by estimating price changes across years only from models in the marketplace whose quality did not change across years; that is, models that were sold in both years. The adequacy of the quality adjustment depends on the degree to which the market for quality is in equilib-

---

30. The prices cited for WordPerfect are the average transactions prices collected by Oliner and Sichel (1994).

31. Formally, this adjustment is done by regressing prices of many products on measures of the processor speed and memory capacity of each product. The coefficients in the regression capture the effect of quality, which can then be used to back out a measure of price change adjusted for quality. See Triplett (1989) for more information.

32. This description of matched-model indexes is taken directly from Oliner and Sichel (1994, p. 299).

rium. If equilibrium prevails, the introduction of a new model or version with a better price-quality trade-off will push down prices of existing models to equalize quality-adjusted prices. In this situation, a matched-model index will correctly capture the change in quality-adjusted prices. Because the required market equilibrium probably does not prevail, matched-model indexes have been criticized for failing to fully adjust for changes in quality. Therefore, these indexes may well understate the true pace of decline in quality-adjusted prices of software.[33]

The above discussion highlights the trade-off between hedonic and matched-model approaches to quality adjustment. In the abstract, most economists would prefer to use hedonic techniques because they provide a direct measure of quality change. Hedonic techniques, however, require identifying and quantifying the set of features that generate value in the marketplace. To the extent that that cannot be accomplished for complex products with a proliferation of features, matched-model techniques might be a plausible alternative.

Price Indexes for PC Applications Software[34]

Erik Brynjolfsson and Chris Kemerer, along with a separate study by Neil Gandal, estimate price indexes for spreadsheets using hedonic techniques, while Oliner and Sichel applied matched-model techniques to spreadsheets, as well as to word processors and database programs. The Brynjolfsson and Kemerer study estimates that quality-adjusted prices of spreadsheets fell at average annual rates ranging from 5 to 12 percent between 1987 and 1992 in nominal terms, depending on the specification used.[35] Gandal's study, using a different set of characteristics to measure quality, finds a somewhat faster decline in spreadsheet prices, averaging about 15 percent a year between 1986 and 1991.[36] As indicated above, however, these studies hinge on identifying the specific characteristics of spreadsheets that generate value in the market, a difficult task for complex and rapidly changing products like spreadsheets.

---

33. For a comparison of hedonic and matched-model price indexes applied to computer hardware see Dulberger (1989).

34. This section draws heavily from Oliner and Sichel (1994), with some text taken directly.

35. Brynjolfsson and Kemerer's preferred model and an alternative generate annual declines of 16 and 9 percent in real terms. To convert these figures to nominal terms, the average annual increase in the GDP deflator, which was 3.9 percent over that period, must be added. Thus the nominal annual price declines ranged from about 12 percent to 5 percent.

36. Gandal (1994, p. 168, table 3).

Table 3-7. *PC Applications Software, Average Price Changes from a Matched-Model Index, 1987–93*

Item	Average price change[a] (annual rate)
Word processors	−1.1
Spreadsheets	−4.0
Database programs	−4.2
Weighted average[b]	−2.7

Source: See table 3A-2.
a. Price changes calculated as log differences times 100.
b. Weighted average calculated using sales weights from table 3A-1.

Although more work needs to be done on hedonic indexes for software, Oliner and Sichel estimated a set of matched-model indexes to provide an alternative starting point.[37] Table 3-7 summarizes their results, showing average price declines from 1987 to 1993 for each product.[38] Spreadsheet prices are estimated to have fallen at an annual rate of 4.0 percent, faster than the estimate obtained by Brynjolfsson and Kemerer but slower than that obtained by Gandal. The pace of price decline for database programs is 4.2 percent, while the rate of price drop for word processors is just 1.1 percent a year. Taking a share-weighted average across all three products, the overall price decline is 2.7 percent a year.

One additional factor is important. As Oliner and Sichel point out, the widespread availability of upgrades, suites, and bundled software may lead their results to understate the pace of decline in the most recent years. They did not include prices of upgrades, products purchased in software "suites," or products bundled with hardware. These alternative sales channels—which have recently become more widespread—probably represent an effective price decline for particular applications. However, such a bias would only appear during the transition from a period when most sales were for new stand-alone products to a period when most purchases were through these other channels.

Overall Software Prices

On the basis of the evidence in these three studies, along with the earlier studies of cost per line of software code written, it appears that

37. To develop the matched-model indexes, Oliner and Sichel collected prices of PC application software for IBM-compatible machines, covering word processing, spreadsheet, and database programs. Transaction prices were pulled from advertisements in computer magazines, including *PC Magazine, Personal Computing, and PC World.*
38. See table 3A-2 in the Appendix to this chapter for details by year and by product.

PC software prices have fallen much more slowly than hardware prices. Even if the pace of decline in software prices from 1987 to 1993 implied by the matched-model indexes were doubled or tripled, it is still well below the 13.5 percent average annual decline in BEA's hardware price index over this period.[39]

Later in this study, the price deflator for PC software will be used as a proxy for the rate of price change of all software, because recent price indexes for overall software are not available. Such an assumption probably is not too unreasonable. The price deflator for PC software fell at an annual rate of 2.7 percent from 1987 to 1993. During this period, the average yearly increase in the GDP deflator was 3.5 percent, implying a real decline in PC software prices of over 6 percent. This figure is close to that suggested by other authors; Gurbaxani suggested a 5 percent annual decline in the real cost of software development, while Phister used a figure of 3.5 percent.[40] These comparisons loosely suggest that using the estimate of PC software prices developed by Oliner and Sichel provides a plausible proxy for the pace of decline in overall software prices.

Casual observation also backs up the implicit assumption that software prices have fallen more slowly than those of hardware, as revealed by the following thought experiment. Compare WordPerfect 6.0 for Windows—first advertised in 1993—to the first DOS version of WordPerfect introduced in 1984. Over this nine-year period, BEA's price index for computers and peripheral equipment implies that a dollar spent on computer hardware in 1993 bought about three and one-half times more firepower than a dollar spent in 1984.[41] Did a dollar spent on software in 1993 also buy three and one-half times more firepower than a dollar spent in 1984? As indicated above, the first DOS version of WordPerfect sold for $277 in March 1984, while version 6.0 for Windows sold for an almost identical price of $276 in December 1993. Would anyone argue that the dollars spent on WordPerfect 6.0 in 1993 bought three and one-half times more writing quality or quantity than the dollars spent on the 1984 version of WordPerfect?[42]

39. Recall that some analysts have suggested that BEA's hardware price index understates the pace of decline in computer hardware prices, in which case software prices would fall even further behind.

40. Gurbaxani (1990); and Phister (1979).

41. BEA's price index for computers and peripheral equipment was 1.581 in 1984 and 0.446 in 1993.

42. This comparison could be done on a real or inflation-adjusted basis by adjusting

Software and the National Income Accounts

Thus far, this chapter has used data from a variety of sources to confirm the important role of software in the economy. Yet, software coverage in the National Income Accounts is limited. In part, this limited coverage reflects the same lack of data that allowed only a limited assessment of software quantities and prices earlier in this chapter. Bringing software more completely into the accounts, however, would greatly facilitate analysts' ability to track this dynamic sector of the economy. This section provides rough quantitative estimates of how the accounts would change if software's coverage were expanded to treat software more similarly to how hardware is covered; namely, to treat more business purchases of software as capitalized assets and to provide additional detail on software elsewhere in the accounts.

Fortunately, the Bureau of Economic Analysis—which publishes the National Accounts—is well aware of these issues and is working to improve the accounts in just the ways described above.[43] To promote their efforts, this section discusses the coverage of software in the accounts and provides rough estimates of how the product side of the accounts would change once software is included in the ways just described.[44]

Business Purchases of Software

As currently defined, GDP equals the sum of personal consumption expenditures by households, business purchases of equipment and structures, business investment in inventories, government purchases of goods and services, and net exports of goods and services. Outside of invento-

---

the computer hardware price index and WordPerfect prices by the overall GDP deflator to take account of overall inflation. Because the general inflation adjustment would be the same for both hardware and software, the comparison of price-quality ratios for hardware and software would tell the same story on a real basis as on the nominal basis in the text.

43. See "Mid-Decade Strategic Review of BEA's Economic Accounts," *Survey of Current Business*, vol. 75 (February 1995), pp. 36–66, especially pp. 62–63.

44. Including software on the product side of the accounts would also necessitate changes on the income side of the accounts. Classifying software as a capital asset would require including depreciation allowances for software in capital consumption and would require making various adjustments to corporate profits. Corporate profits would be adjusted upward because software would no longer be an intermediate input that is fully expensed. At the same time, corporate profits would be adjusted somewhat downward because charges for depreciation would be higher once software were included.

ries, business spending in GDP only includes purchases of capital goods. Other inputs purchased by businesses—including such items as pencils, energy inputs, and banking services—are not directly included to avoid double counting. The value of these inputs gets into GDP indirectly; for example, if a household buys a car, then the value of the car already embodies the value of the inputs used by the manufacturer to produce it. To avoid double counting, inputs that are used up in the production of the car are not counted separately in GDP.

As indicated, capital goods are handled differently in the National Accounts than other inputs. The physical plant used to produce the car lasts a long time and is not completely used up in the production of the car in the way electricity is. Thus business purchases of physical capital are counted directly in GDP. Primarily, business investment in the National Accounts includes purchases of physical equipment and structures—things that would hurt if dropped on one's foot—although some nonphysical expenditures are also included.[45] And currently, software purchased separately is not considered a capital good, even though software lasts a long time and is not used up in the production of other items as is, say, electricity. (If businesses purchase software that is bundled with hardware, the accounts do not separate the value of the bundled software, counting the entire purchase in the hardware category. Therefore, these purchases of bundled software are counted as capitalized assets.)

Whether or not software should be counted as a capital good raises the more general question of how to define capital goods. Businesses invest in many nonphysical assets that pay off far in the future, including advertising, research and development, and worker and manager training. Purchases of these assets have not been considered business investment in the National Accounts even though such purchases may provide a service flow over many years.[46] And, over on the household side of the accounts, purchases of education—referred to by economists as human capital—are counted as consumption rather than investment. Whether or not the definition of capital should be extended to include these other items is an open and complicated question. But, because software lasts a long time and is so closely tied to computer hardware, it makes little sense not to count software as a capital good.

45. Examples of these nonphysical expenditures include development and exploration expenses for oil, gas, and other minerals, and all services associated with the purchase of equipment and structures, including legal and architectural services.
46. Although not part of the official accounting of GDP, BEA does publish satellite accounts for research and development.

Software Elsewhere in the Accounts

As described above, many business purchases of software are not counted as GDP. Elsewhere in the accounts, expenditures for software largely do get into GDP, but they are are not broken out separately and are included in broader categories, often because data limitations make a detailed breakout difficult. Including software in broader categories creates two difficulties. First, the lack of detail makes it impossible to track purchases of software in the economy. Tracking software more closely would be a big plus since this industry is growing rapidly and is a leading sector in the U.S. economy. Second, including software in a broader category with other items leads to a misstatement of real, or inflation-adjusted, GDP. As indicated, various purchases of software get counted in nominal GDP. However, because they are included in broader categories with other items, the wrong deflator is used to convert nominal spending to real purchases, leading to mismeasurement of real GDP.

What If the National Accounts Covered Software More Comprehensively?

Table 3-8 shows nominal GDP for 1993 under the current accounting rules and under alternative accounting rules in which software is included as a capital good and detail for software purchases is broken out. The table divides nominal GDP into its major components (consumption, investment, government spending, and net exports), and divides spending within each component among hardware, software, and other investment.[47] The first column of the table adds up the major components of GDP under current accounting rules. Because software is not counted as a capital good, the software piece of equipment investment is zero.[48] And, because software is included in broader categories elsewhere in the accounts, the software pieces of those other sectors also is recorded as zero in table 3-8.

The second column of the table adds up the major components of nominal GDP under alternative accounting rules, in which software is

47. BEA publishes detail on hardware for exports, imports, and investment. For investment the category is computers and peripheral equipment. For exports and imports, the category also includes parts. For example, see *Survey of Current Business*, vol. 74 (July 1994). For the other major sectors—consumption and government—the hardware detail is taken from unpublished BEA data.

48. As indicated earlier, a portion of business investment in hardware covers software that is bundled with the hardware.

Table 3-8. *Nominal Software in the National Income and Product Accounts, 1993*

Billions of nominal dollars

Item	Current accounting	Including software	Difference
Consumption			
Hardware	7.7	7.7	0.0
Software	0.0	1.5	1.5
Other	4370.5	4369.0	−1.5
Equipment investment			
Hardware	47.0	47.0	0.0
Software	0.0	35.2	35.2
Other	395.7	395.7	0.0
Other investment	439.4	439.4	0.0
Government			
Hardware	2.7	2.7	0.0
Software	0.0	0.5	0.5
Other	1145.7	1145.2	−0.5
Exports			
Hardware	29.3	29.3	0.0
Software	0.0	5.6	5.6
Other	629.8	624.2	−5.6
Imports	724.3	724.3	0.0
Hardware	38.0	38.0	0.0
Software	0.0	0.0	0.0
Other	686.3	686.3	0.0
GDP	6343.5	6378.6	35.2

Source: U.S. Department of Commerce, *Survey of Current Business* (July 1994) and unpublished data; U.S. Department of Commerce, *Current Business Reports: Service Annual Survey* (1993); and author's calculations as described in the text.

defined as a capital good and in which detail for software is broken out. The figures for software spending within each component are obtained by allocating the Census Bureau's 1993 figure for revenue in the software industry. As reported in table 3-4, this figure is $42.8 billion.[49] Recall that this figure covers a relatively narrow definition of software, including prepackaged software and programming services; it does not include software maintenance and development costs done directly by users. Although these latter software expenses could be included in principle, there is little hope that BEA could obtain data of sufficient quality to do so.

49. For 1993 prepackaged software accounted for $16.7 billion of the $42.8 billion total, while programming services made up the remaining $26.1 billion.

Even allocating software industry revenues from the Census Bureau requires detailed data that are difficult to gather; hence, the difficulty of the task faced by BEA. To obtain the crude recalculation shown in the second column of table 3-8, three assumptions are made about software purchases. As will be plainly apparent, none of these assumptions is literally correct, but they do provide a basis for a first-cut allocation of software spending. First, all purchases of programming services are counted as business investment. Second, prepackaged software is allocated in proportion to hardware purchases by businesses, households, the government, and foreigners. Third, imports of software are assumed to be zero.[50]

The second column of table 3-8 differs from the first in three important ways. First, nominal equipment investment is higher by $35.2 billion, the estimated amount of business software purchases. This increment boosts the level of nominal equipment investment by almost 8 percent.[51] Second, software is now broken out from the "other" components in consumption, government, and exports. But the increments in software are exactly offset by decreases in the "other" categories. Moreover, within these other broad sectors of GDP, the increments for software are much smaller than for equipment investment. Third, nominal GDP is higher by $35.2 billion, or about one-half of 1 percent. Note that the boost to nominal GDP exactly equals the increment to nominal equipment investment, because the detail on software elsewhere only represents a reallocation from the "other" categories.

Table 3-9 repeats table 3-8, but in 1987 constant dollars rather than in nominal terms. The constant-dollar figures were calculated by deflating the figures in table 3-8 with the deflators shown in the fourth column of table 3-9.[52] Again, the alternative accounting procedures lead to three

50. Although not literally true, this assumption about imports probably is roughly reasonable. According to the OECD (1994, p. 29) U.S. companies produced 97 percent of the packaged software purchased in the United States in 1991.

51. This figure probably overstates software's increment to equipment investment. Sales of firms primarily selling prepackaged software include sales of software that is bundled with hardware. As indicated earlier, bundled software is already counted in business investment. In principle, software's increment to nominal equipment investment should be marked down by this amount of double counting. The potential amount of double counting, however, is not that large. In table 3-8, of the $16.7 billion of prepackaged software sales in 1993, $9.1 billion was allocated to equipment investment. Although little information is available on the amount of bundled software purchased, suppose half of the $9.1 billion figure reflected bundled sales. Then software's increment to nominal equipment investment would only be marked down from $35.2 billion to $30.7 billion [= 35.2 − (9.1/2)].

52. The deflators shown in the fourth column are used to obtain constant-dollar figures

Table 3-9. *Real Software in the National Income and Product Accounts, 1993*

Billions of 1987 dollars

Item	Current accounting	Including software	Difference	Deflators (1987 = 100)
Consumption				
Hardware	21.0	21.0	0.0	0.37
Software	0.0	1.7	1.7	0.85
Other	3437.7	3436.5	−1.2	1.27
Equipment investment				
Hardware	105.4	105.4	0.0	0.45
Software	0.0	41.3	41.3	0.85
Other	338.5	338.5	0.0	1.17
Other investment	376.0	376.0	0.0	1.09
Government				
Hardware	6.1	6.1	0.0	0.50
Software	0.0	0.6	0.6	0.85
Other	923.7	923.3	−0.4	1.24
Exports				
Hardware	66.6	66.6	0.0	0.44
Software	0.0	6.6	6.6	0.85
Other	535.9	531.1	−4.8	1.18
Imports	724.3	724.3	0.0	1.07
GDP	5134.6	5178.5	43.9	

Source: See table 3-8. Software deflator from table 3A-2.

primary changes in the accounts on a constant-dollar basis. First, real equipment investment is $41.3 billion higher under the alternative procedures that include software, boosting the level of real equipment investment by more than 9 percent. Second—in contrast to the nominal figures—real GDP is boosted in other major sectors. This occurs because the deflator for software is lower than the deflators for the "other" categories. Thus the reallocations from "other" to software that are offset exactly in nominal terms imply a larger increment to real software spending in these categories than the decrement to real "other" spending. Third, adding in software boosts real GDP by $43.9 billion, or more than three-quarters of a percent of GDP.

---

for both the current accounting rules and the alternative procedure that includes software. Technically, the deflator for "other" consumption, "other" government, and "other" exports would differ slightly under the two accounting procedures. For simplicity and transparency, these differences are ignored.

Table 3-10. *Growth Rate of Software in the National Income and Product Accounts, 1991–93*

	Levels (billions of dollars)			Growth rates (percent)		
Year	Current accounting	Including software	Software	Current accounting	Including software	Software
	Nominal business investment in equipment and software					
1990	385.1	410.9	25.8			
1991	374.1	401.0	27.9	−2.9	−2.2	8.1
1992	390.3	420.5	30.2	4.3	4.6	8.2
1993	442.7	477.9	35.2	13.4	13.6	16.4
	Real business investment in equipment and software (1987 dollars)					
1990	356.0	394.8	27.8			
1991	354.9	385.4	30.5	−3.3	−2.7	9.8
1992	376.2	411.4	35.2	6.0	6.8	15.5
1993	443.9	485.2	41.3	18.0	17.9	17.3
	Nominal GDP					
1990	5546.1	5571.9	25.8			
1991	5724.8	5752.7	27.9	3.2	3.2	8.1
1992	6020.1	6050.3	30.2	5.2	5.2	8.2
1993	6343.5	6378.7	35.2	5.4	5.4	16.4
	Real GDP (1987 dollars)					
1990	4897.3	4926.1	28.8			
1991	4867.8	4899.8	32.0	−0.6	−0.5	11.1
1992	4979.4	5017.0	37.6	2.3	2.4	17.8
1993	5134.6	5178.5	43.9	3.1	3.2	17.0

Source: See tables 3-8, 3-9.

As just shown, including software boosts the level of real equipment investment and of real GDP. It would also change growth rates if software purchases grew at a different rate than other real equipment investment or real GDP. From 1991 to 1993, table 3-10 shows growth rates for GDP and equipment investment once software is included.[53] The nominal and real figures including software were calculated in exactly the manner used for tables 3-8 and 3-9. As table 3-10 shows, including software boosts both nominal and real investment notably. Because software purchases grew rapidly, annual growth rates for real business investment in equipment and software are generally higher by about three-fourths of a percentage point.[54]

53. The U.S Department of Commerce, *Current Business Reports: Service Annual Survey* (1993) only includes sufficient detail beginning in 1990; therefore, growth rates can only be calculated starting in 1991.

54. In 1993 growth of real business investment in equipment and software is actually a tad slower once software is included. This occurs because equipment investment grew more rapidly than software investment in that year.

For real GDP growth, the inclusion of software in the accounts has a relatively small impact. While the level of both nominal and real GDP is higher once software is included, software's share of GDP is just too small to have much impact on overall GDP growth rates. For real GDP growth, including software boosts annual growth by about 0.1 percentage point.

Computing Services

As indicated earlier, businesses are interested in the "computing services" flowing from their information technology, and computing services are the joint product of hardware, software, and labor inputs. To focus on computing services, hardware, software, and labor inputs must be combined, which requires information on their relative shares as inputs. This section starts with those input shares. The combination of these inputs on the quantity side—to assess the contribution of computing services to output growth—is postponed until chapter 4. This section does, however, combine these inputs on the price side to construct a price index for computing services. Finally, this section compares purchases of computing services across the United States, Japan, and Europe.

Hardware, Software, and Labor Shares

Based on surveys of information system departments of large U.S. companies between 1976 and 1984, Gurbaxani estimated budget shares for hardware, software, and other expenses including labor.[55] Of these budgets, hardware accounted for 38 percent, software for 28 percent, and labor and other expenses 34 percent. According to these figures, hardware accounts for a bit more than a third of spending on information systems, while software accounts for somewhat less than a third. Put another way, software purchases were about 74 percent of hardware purchases (0.74 = 0.28/0.38), while purchases of labor and other inputs were about 89 percent of hardware purchases (0.89 = 0.34/0.38). Gurbaxani reports that these budget shares were quite stable from 1976 to 1984.

---

55. Gurbaxani (1990, pp. 63–66). The budget share outside of hardware and software is attributed to computer-services labor.

As for more recent estimates of these shares, an illustrative calculation suggests that Gurbaxani's shares remain in a reasonable ballpark. Specifically, the data on hardware and software in table 3-8 for 1993 provide another view of the relative shares of hardware and software purchased by the business sector. Total purchases of hardware by the business sector were $47.0 billion and total purchases of software were estimated to be $35.2 billion.[56] These figures imply that software purchases were 75 percent of hardware purchases, about the same as the 74 percent implied by Gurbaxani's numbers.

Although Gurbaxani's shares will be used for calculations throughout the rest of the book, it is important to emphasize the roughness of these estimates of input shares. A recent OECD study reported that hardware and software purchases in the United States were nearly equal in 1993, implying a higher share for software than reported by Gurbaxani.[57] On the other hand, there are reasons to suspect that the increased use of PCs might have reduced the software share as businesses purchase more software with site licenses, lowering the price of software installed per PC.

A Rough Measure of Price Change for Computing Services

With these input shares, a rough price index for computing services can be calculated. Table 3-11 brings together the essential elements for this calculation. The input shares shown are those discussed above, as reported by Gurbaxani. The second column of the table reports estimated average rates of price change for each of the three components of computing services from 1987 to 1993. For hardware, the price index is BEA's measure for computers and peripheral equipment. For software, the rate of price change or PC applications software is taken from table 3-7. As indicated earlier, this price index for PC applications software is not the ideal index to use for all software, but it provides a plausible estimate. Because a price index for computing-services labor is not available, an index of overall labor costs is shown in the third row of the table, on the assumption that wages for computing-services workers increased at the same rate as overall wages.

---

56. These figures for total purchases by the business sector are from the equipment investment panel of table 3-8.

57. The OECD study reported for 1993 that hardware spending in the United States was approximately $63 billion and that software spending was about $62 billion, implying that software and hardware purchases are nearly equal. See OECD (1994, figure 12, p. 23; figure 16, p. 26).

Table 3-11. *Average Annual Price Change for Computing Services, 1987–93*

Component	Share (percent)[a]	Average annual price change (percent)[b]
(1) Hardware	38	− 13.5
(2) Software	28	− 2.7
(3) Computer-services labor	34	4.3
(4) Computing services[c]	100	− 4.4

Addendum

(5) GDP deflator		3.5
(6) Real price of computing services[d]		− 7.9
(7) Real price of hardware[e]		− 17.0

Source: Hardware prices are based on BEA's index for computer and peripheral equipment described earlier. Software prices are based on the matched-model index for PC Applications software from Oliner and Sichel (1994). Labor costs are based on the Employment Cost Index published by the Bureau of Labor Statistics. The GDP deflator is from U.S. Department of Labor (1993).
a. Shares from Gurbaxani (1990).
b. Average log difference times 100.
c. Weighted average of price changes in lines (1) to (3) using shares as weights.
d. Price change for computing services minus change in GDP deflator.
e. Price change for hardware minus change in GDP deflator.

Using the input share weights, the fourth line of table 3-11 reports that the overall price of computing services—including hardware, software, and labor inputs—fell at an annual rate of 4.4 percent between 1987 and 1993. Looked at through the prism of computing services, the pace of technical advance for the entire computing package, as actually used, is much slower than the 13.5 percent annual decline reported for hardware alone over this period. Chapter 5 shows that the pace of price decline for computing services has parallels to other products in earlier periods of innovation.

The Intensity of Computing Services across Countries

Suppose that among countries with similar economies, some were substantially more computer-intensive than others. Implicitly, these countries are betting that a more technology-intensive strategy will generate larger payoffs and perhaps faster future growth than alternative strategies pursued by other industrialized nations.

Cross-country comparisons are extremely difficult because of limited data availability and noncomparability across countries. A recent OECD report, however, provides some guidance on purchases of information technology as a share of GDP. Table 3-12 reports these shares for the

Table 3-12. *Spending on Information Technology in the United States, Japan, and Europe, 1986, 1990, 1993*

Nominal GDP shares, percent

Region	1986	1990	1993
United States	2.0	2.3	2.4
Japan	1.4	2.0	1.6
Europe	1.4	2.3	1.8

Source: OECD (1994, fig. 1, p. 16). In the OECD data, information technology includes computer hardware, software, computer support services, and communication equipment linked and used specifically with computer devices.

United States, Japan, and Europe in three different years.[58] In 1993 the United States spent about two and one-half percent of its GDP on information technology, almost one percentage point more of GDP on information technology than Japan and about one-half percentage point more than Europe. Back in 1990, when a recession held down the share in the United States, the shares were more nearly equal. But back in 1986 the United States spent a significantly larger share than Japan or Europe. On balance, these figures suggest that the United States is somewhat more heavily dedicated to an information-technology strategy than its competitors.

Appendix: Capital Stocks for Computers and Peripheral Equipment (CPE)

BEA has published real and nominal investment data for computers and peripheral equipment (CPE) back to 1982.[59] Earlier data are unpublished but available back to 1959. Oliner and Sichel constructed net capital stock and capital input stock for CPE—reals and nominals—in exactly the manner used by BEA to construct stocks for office, computing, and accounting equipment (OCA).[60] For example, to get real OCA net capital

58. The OECD definition of information technology covers more than just computer hardware, including hardware, software, support services, and communication devices that link and are used specifically with computing devices.

59. This section of the Appendix is reproduced directly from Oliner and Sichel (1994, pp. 315–16), with only minor changes.

60. Besides net capital stocks, BEA publishes capital input stocks and gross capital stocks. The net stock measures the market value of the capital stock under the assumption of straightline depreciation, while the capital input stock is designed to measure the service flow from the capital stock. The gross stock also is designed to capture service flows, but with a different set of decay assumptions than the capital input series.

stock, BEA takes a weighted average of current and past real gross investment, with the weights reflecting the decay path of OCA over time. For real OCA capital input, BEA uses the same procedure with slightly different weights. To construct stocks for CPE, the weights used by BEA for OCA were used. Analogous to BEA procedures, nominal stocks are constructed by applying deflators to the real series.[61]

The stocks for CPE have the virtue of focusing just on computers. However, because BEA does not publish the investment data for CPE before 1982, questions have been raised about the quality of the earlier data. More specifically, from the early 1970s forward, the investment data for CPE are of reasonably high quality because there is sufficient detail on manufacturers' shipments of OCA to break out CPE. Before 1972, however, the shipments data are more highly aggregated and the decomposition into CPE is more judgmental. BEA tapers this series down to zero in 1958, a year in which computers were clearly used in the business sector. Although these lower-quality investment data are potentially problematic, their influence on capital stocks quickly wanes after 1972 for two reasons. First, computers have short service lives. Thus, just a few years beyond 1972, the earlier vintages already have a low weight in the capital stock. Second, investment in CPE grows rapidly after 1972, implying that newer vintages are a much bigger portion of capital stock measures than the earlier, more problematic, vintages.

Real and Nominal Measures of Computers and Their Uses

As indicated in the text, real constant-dollar measures of computers or output expressed in constant dollars are inappropriate for certain uses. These real measures use prices from a base year to calculate constant-dollar (or fixed-weight) output in other years. If relative prices change

---

61. As indicated, the real net capital stock series shown in figure 1-2 was calculated by taking a weighted average of real investment in computers and peripheral equipment (CPE), where the weights are BEA's decay weights for office, computing, and accounting equipment. Oliner and Sichel (1994) calculated this series through 1993. The series in figure 1-2 was extended to 1994 and 1995 by extending their calculation to include estimates of real investment in CPE in 1987 dollars for 1994 and 1995. The estimate of real investment in CPE in 1987 dollars for 1994 was taken from *Survey of Current Business*, vol. 75 (August 1995). Because BEA recently switched to 1992 chain weights, BEA never published an estimate of CPE for 1995 in 1987 dollars. To generate such an estimate, the 1995 growth rate of CPE in 1992 chain dollars was used to grow out the 1994 figure for CPE in 1987 dollars. The figures for CPE in 1995 were taken from *Survey of Current Business*, vol. 76 (August 1996).

over time, these constant-dollar measures are misleading because of their reliance on base-year prices, which were not actually faced by consumers or producers in other years. For example, computer prices have fallen rapidly over time. A measure of real GDP for 1994 based on prices from a 1987 base year will use computer prices that are much higher than those that actually prevailed in 1994. Thus the value of real output will be overstated when evaluated at the much higher, and out of date, computer prices. This type of distortion is referred to by economists and statisticians as an "index-number" problem.

The index-number problem can be understood intuitively by focusing on the arbitrary choice of base years for constant-dollar measures. For example, one could just as well choose 1970 as a base year. In that year, computers were much more expensive than in later years. Thus, real output growth in 1994—calculated in the prices of 1970—would place an even larger weight on computers and would be even more overstated. Alternatively, one could use prices expected to prevail in the year 2000 as base year prices. Because computer prices are likely to fall further, this would put a smaller weight on computers, pulling down the constant-dollar measure of real output growth in 1994 and understating true output growth.

To be more precise, this Appendix presents two examples of how index-number problems can lead to biases in constant-dollar measures of computers and output. The examples focus on GDP and its components, but the relationships shown would be identical for capital stock series.

Constant-Dollar Output

Let Y equal constant-dollar output consisting of two components, computers and all other items, denoted by C and O, respectively. Let the 1987 base year price of computers equal P_{87}^C and the price of all other items be P_{87}^O. Then constant-dollar output can be expressed as:

$$(3A\text{-}1) \qquad Y = P_{87}^C C + P_{87}^O O.$$

Let variables with dots over them represent growth rates. With a little algebra, it is easy to show that the growth rate of constant-dollar output equals a weighted average of growth rates of computers and everything else. Namely,

(3A-2) $\dot{Y} = P_{87}^C (C_{-1}/Y_{-1})\dot{C} + P_{87}^O (O_{-1}/Y_{-1})\dot{O}.$

In equation 3A-2, the weights on growth in computers ($\dot{C}$) and everything else ($\dot{O}$) equal the real share lagged one period multiplied by the base year price of each item.

In the base year 1987, the prices, P_{87}^C and P_{87}^O, accurately reflect prices that prevailed in 1987. Now consider 1994. By that time computer prices had fallen substantially, but the base year price for computers, P_{87}^C, would not reflect this. And because the base year price is much higher than the price in 1994, the constant-dollar output formula in equation 3A-2 would put too much weight on the growth of computers by 1994. Because, growth in computer purchases ($\dot{C}$) has been so much more rapid than growth in other purchases ($\dot{O}$), equation 3A-2 would be putting too much weight on the fastest growing component. Thus, the constant-dollar measure of output growth would overstate true output growth in 1994.

To overcome this difficulty, BEA recently began publishing alternative measures of real output that allow the aggregation weights to change gradually over time to account for changes in the structure of the economy over time. These measures are called chain-weight indexes because they chain together aggregation weights from different years, rather than using a single year's weights as in the constant-dollar measures.[62]

Constant-Dollar Output Shares

Constant-dollar output measures are also problematic for computing output shares. For example, consider the real share of computers in output measured in constant dollars. This share can be represented as:

(3A-3) $P_{87}^C C/Y = P_{87}^C C \,/\, (P_{87}^C C + P_{87}^O O).$

In 1987 this constant-dollar share will be accurate, but by 1994 it will not be. Suppose for this example that computer prices had fallen 50 percent by 1994 and that other prices had not changed. Then by 1994, the numerator in equation 3A-3 would be 50 percent higher than if 1994 prices were used. The denominator would also be larger than if 1994 prices were used, but by less than 50 percent because the overstatement of computer prices only affects the first term in the denominator on the

---

62. For more detail, see *Survey of Current Business*, vol. 72 (April and November 1992).

Table 3A-1. *Nominal Sales of PC Applications Software*

Millions of dollars unless noted otherwise

Year	Total	Word processors	Spreadsheets	Databases
1987	2,313.0	339.3	344.7	207.2
1988	3,247.5	499.5	442.9	337.7
1989	3,633.9	686.3	571.4	318.0
1990	4,585.8	917.9	703.1	345.0
1991[a] (old basis)	5,713.2	1,136.0	946.7	396.8
1991[a] (new basis)	5,063.6	812.4	739.1	309.7
1992	5,745.4	829.5	795.3	348.5
1993	6,809.6	1,021.6	801.2	475.5
	Annual growth rates (log differences times 100)			
1988	33.9	38.7	25.1	48.8
1989	11.2	31.8	25.5	−6.0
1990	23.3	29.1	20.5	8.2
1991	22.0	21.3	30.0	14.0
1992	13.2	2.1	7.3	11.8
1993	17.0	20.8	.7	31.1
Average				
1988–93	20.1	24.0	18.2	18.0

Source: Software Publishers Association (SPA), various press releases, Washington, D.C.

a. In 1991, the SPA revamped their data procedures, yielding two sets of figures for 1991. The figures labeled "new basis" are comparable to the later figures, while the "old basis" figures are comparable to the earlier data. Total includes miscellaneous PC Applications software not shown in the table.

right-hand side of the equation. Thus the full expression in equation 3A-3 would overstate the real share of computers because the overstatement in the numerator would exceed the overstatement in the denominator.

Nominal Output Shares

In contrast to constant-dollar shares, nominal shares are not misleading because there is no adjustment to base-year prices. For example, the nominal computer share in GDP shows the share of output allocated to computers in a year in the prices that actually prevailed in that year. Throughout the book, shares involving computers are shown in nominal terms whenever possible. As is clear from the discussion in chapter 2, nominal shares also turn out to be the right share to use for growth accounting.

Another Exception

These examples indicate that certain constant-dollar series can be misleading when aggregating across components that have undergone

Table 3A-2. *PC Applications Software, Annual Matched-Model Price Changes*

Log differences times 100

Year	Word processors	Spreadsheets	Database programs	Total
1986	−11.4	−9.9	−11.3	—
1987	−2.7	−1.9	−1.0	−2.0
1988	−.4	−1.5	−3.0	−1.5
1989	3.4	−7.5	−4.2	−2.1
1990	−1.3	−4.4	−8.8	−3.7
1991	−1.9	2.5	−10.5	−1.6
1992	−6.4	−9.1	−1.0	−6.5
1993	.1	−4.0	2.6	−.8
Average annual change (1987–93)	−1.1	−4.0	−4.2	−2.7

Addendum

Price index for total PC Applications software (1987 = 100)[a]

1987	1988	1989	1990	1991	1992	1993
1.00	0.985	0.965	0.930	0.915	0.857	0.850

Source: Oliner and Sichel (1994). The index for the total is a weighted average of the first three columns, using the weights implicit in the nominal sales figures shown in table 3A-1.

a. The price index is calculated by setting 1987 equal to ln(100), decrementing by each year's total log difference, exponentiating the resulting series, and dividing by 100.

changes in relative prices or when focusing on the level or share of a constant-dollar series. However, *rates of change* of constant-dollar measures at the most highly disaggregated level are not affected by changes in relative prices because there is no aggregation across items whose relative prices can change. Even at the most highly disaggregated level of detail, the level of a constant-dollar series is affected by the choice of base year, but growth rates are not. Therefore, calculating growth rates from constant-dollar series at the finest level of detail avoids biases. Of BEA's published series for investment, CPE is at the finest level of disaggregation. Thus it is reasonable to calculate growth rates of real investment in CPE from the constant-dollar measure.[63]

The same point can be made intuitively by considering alternative base years. If CPE is rebased to 1992 dollars, growth rates in the series in

63. Even at this level, there are still minor problems because BEA constructs the CPE investment series by aggregating series for computers and series for peripherals. The problems, however, are unlikely to be too severe because the relative price changes within CPE probably are not too dramatic.

1992 dollars will be nearly the same as growth rates in CPE on a 1987-dollar basis, even though the level of the series will be different for each base year.[64] Thus, in many places throughout the book, growth rates of real investment in CPE or real capital stock of CPE are calculated from the constant-dollar figures.

64. Subject to the qualification explained in note 63.

CHAPTER 4

Measuring the Aggregate Impact
of Computers

$\mathbf{B}$ECAUSE MUCH previous work has focused on computer hardware, and because the most complete data exist for hardware, this chapter starts by estimating the contribution of computer hardware to economic growth. The analytic framework developed in chapter 2 is used. A later section of this chapter expands the framework to computing services, including software and computer-related labor in the calculations. Empirical measures of economic welfare, including the contribution of computing services to net output and consumer surplus, are also discussed. Then I consider how much more computing services would contribute to growth if hardware and software earned a better-than-competitive return. The impact of measurement error on the growth-accounting estimates is explained, and finally I roll the clock forward, establishing a plausible range for future contributions of computing services to overall economic growth and establishing what would have to occur for these growth contributions to increase significantly in coming years.

Computer Hardware and Economic Growth

Although later sections in this chapter consider the broader category of computing services, this section starts with computer hardware, providing an analytic base to which the other elements of computing services can be added. Because of better data availability for hardware, the analysis can be extended further back in time for hardware than for computing services.[1]

---

1. This chapter draws heavily on Oliner and Sichel (1994).

Baseline Neoclassical Contribution

As mentioned earlier, Edward F. Denison was the first to decompose the growth of real output into the contribution from the growth of each input, typically focusing on capital and labor. Stephen D. Oliner and Daniel E. Sichel extended Denison's work by separating computers from the rest of capital.[2] They developed the following decomposition of output growth, which is derived formally in the Appendix to this chapter:

(output growth) = (neoclassical contribution of growth in computer
                 capital)

           + (neoclassical contribution of growth in the stock of
                 all other capital)

(4-1)   + (neoclassical contribution of labor growth)

           + (contribution of multifactor productivity growth).

The first term on the right-hand side of equation 4-1 corresponds to the term for the neoclassical contribution of computers from equation 2-2. The next two terms on the right-hand side of equation 4-1 represent the neoclassical contributions to output growth of other capital and labor; that is, the contributions assuming that these factors are paid competitive returns.[3]

The multifactor productivity (MFP) term identifies the portion of output growth after accounting for growth in capital and labor; that is, MFP is a catchall for every source of growth over and above the neoclassical contributions of computers, other capital, and labor. It reflects technological or organizational improvements in the efficiency of translating inputs into output. Because only the neoclassical contribution of computers appears explicitly in equation 4-1, any excess contribution accruing if computers earn supernormal returns has been absorbed into the MFP term. The possible magnitude of such supernormal returns is discussed later in this chapter under "Mismeasurement of Output."

How big are the different contributions to output growth in the decomposition in equation 4-1? Table 4-1 shows Oliner and Sichel's estimates of the terms in equation 4-1 over three time periods, 1970–92,

Table 4-1. *Contributions to Growth of Real Gross Output of Private Nonfarm Business, 1970–92*

Measure	1970–92	1970–79	1980–92
Growth rate of output[a]	2.8	3.4	2.3
Contributions from[b]			
Computer hardware	0.15	0.09	0.20
Other capital	1.00	1.17	.89
Labor hours	.95	1.17	.79
Multifactor productivity	.67	.99	.42
Income shares[c]			
Computer hardware	0.6	0.3	0.8
Other capital	29.1	28.8	29.3
Labor hours	70.3	70.9	69.9
Growth of inputs[a]			
Computer hardware	26.9	27.5	26.5
Other capital	3.5	4.1	3.0
Labor hours	1.4	1.7	1.1

Source: Oliner and Sichel (1994, table 3). Figures for computing equipment differ slightly from Oliner and Sichel, reflecting correction of a minor programming error.
a. Average annual log difference multiplied by 100.
b. Percentage points a year.
c. Percent.

1970–79, and 1980–92. Recall that these estimates are based on the assumption that computers earn the same competitive net return as other capital investments. As indicated in chapter 2, Oliner and Sichel estimated that the competitive net return to all nonresidential equipment and structures is about 12 percent in nominal terms. To this figure, about a 25 percent depreciation rate is added for computer hardware, yielding a gross return to computers of about 37 percent. These are the returns on which the following growth contributions are based.

The central result revealed by table 4-1 is that computer hardware has made a small contribution to growth.[4] Between 1970 and 1992 output growth averaged 2.8 percent.[5] Of this growth, computers contributed only 0.15 percentage point annually to the growth of business output, as

4. This paragraph and the following two are taken almost directly from Oliner and Sichel (1994, pp. 283–84).
5. The output measure used to obtain the figures in table 4-1 is gross business output for the private nonfarm business sector, which excludes the output of farms and the government. These sectors are typically excluded in analyses of business productivity. The output measure used is a Fisher Ideal Index and the real capital stock measures are Tornquist indexes, both prepared by the U.S. Dept. of Labor, Bureau of Labor Statistics (1983, 1993). Just like the alternative output indexes that BEA recently began publishing, the Fisher Ideal Index and the Tornquist index take account of changes in relative prices over time and therefore are not subject to the index-number problems described in chapter 3.

shown on the second line of the table. In the more recent period, 1980 to 1992, the contribution of computers is more than double that in the preceding decade, but still is only 0.20 percentage point a year. Although an extra couple of tenths of a percentage point of growth a year would cumulate substantially over many years, it remains quite small compared with the productivity slowdown of about one and one-half percentage point in the 1970s.[6] Finally, note that although these estimates are calculated in terms of output growth, they translate directly into estimates of the impact on growth in labor productivity. For a given quantity of labor, more output growth implies an equal increment to productivity growth.

The lower part of the table explains why computer hardware has had so little effect on growth. Recall from chapter 2 that the growth contribution of any input equals its nominal income share multiplied by the growth rate of the real stock of the input. For computing equipment, the real capital input stock has grown extremely rapidly—at an average annual rate of 26.9 percent between 1970 and 1992. However, the share of nominal income accruing to computer hardware remains negligible. This income share averaged only 0.6 percent between 1970 and 1992, and although it generally rose over the sample period, its maximum value was only 1.1 percent, attained in 1989. This share remained small because the stock of computer hardware continues to represent a tiny fraction of the nominal capital stock in the United States, accounting for less than 2 percent of the nominal net stock of private nonresidential equipment and structures in 1993.[7]

Furthermore, the contribution of computer hardware is swamped by that of noncomputer capital. As table 4-1 also shows, the contribution from capital other than computers averaged 1.0 percentage point a year over 1970–92, more than six times the contribution from computers. Moreover, figure 4-1 shows that the growth contribution of noncomputer capital shrank since 1980, more than offsetting the increase in the contribution of computers. This dropback in the contribution of other capital provides another reason why productivity growth remained sluggish in the 1980s: as firms boosted their purchases of computers, they scaled back investments in other capital.

6. Denison (1985, p. 35).
7. David Romer hinted at this explanation in his comment on Baily and Gordon (1988, p. 427), as did Brynjolfsson (1993).

Figure 4-1. *Growth Contributions, Computers and Other Capital*

Percentage points a year

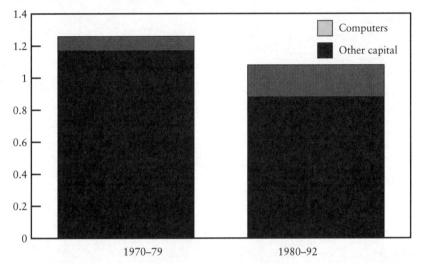

Source: Growth contributions from table 4-1. Procedures used are described in the text.

Recall from the discussion in chapter 2 that one explanation offered for the productivity paradox was the offsetting-factors hypothesis; that is, other factors have dragged down growth in a way that has masked the contribution of computing services. Although the dropback in the contribution of noncomputer capital was modest between the 1970s and 1980s, this dropback does provide an example of a noncomputer factor offsetting an increase in the contribution of computer hardware.

Computing Services and Economic Growth

As indicated earlier, hardware cannot be used in isolation. Ultimately, businesses are interested in the "computing services" flowing from their information technology, and computing services are the joint product of hardware, software, and labor inputs. Thus, the growth-accounting calculations in the last section should be extended to include software and labor inputs. As described below, Oliner and Sichel do just such a calculation for the period from 1987 to 1993.[8]

8. Oliner and Sichel (1994, p. 296).

Table 4-2. *Contributions of Computing Services to Growth in Gross and Net Output, 1987–93*

Item	Gross output	Net output
Contributions from[a]		
Computing services	0.31	0.15
Computer hardware	0.15	0.06
Computer software	0.11	0.04
Computer labor	0.05	0.05
Income shares[b]		
Computing services	2.4	1.4
Computer hardware	0.9	0.3
Computer software	0.7	0.3
Computer labor	0.8	0.9
Growth of inputs[c]		
Computer hardware	17.2	17.2
Computer software	15.3	15.3
Computer labor	6.0	6.0
Addendum		
Growth of output (percent a year)	2.0	1.6

Source: Oliner and Sichel (1994, table 9); and author's calculations as described in the text. Figures here differ slightly from those in Oliner and Sichel, reflecting correction of a minor programming error.
a. Percentage point a year.
b. Percent.
c. Percent. Average log differences multiplied by 100.

To extend the basic growth-accounting relationship, Oliner and Sichel add a term for the contribution of software to the growth-accounting relationship and strip out computer-related labor from the rest of labor input. Then the contribution of computing services to output growth can be expressed as:[9]

(4-2)

Contribution of computing services to output growth =
(hardware contribution) +
(software contribution) +
(computer-services labor contribution).

The hardware contribution is calculated in the same way as it was earlier. To calculate the software and computer-services labor contributions, it is necessary to know the real growth rates of each of these inputs and their importance relative to hardware. Table 4-2 brings together the essential elements for the extended growth-accounting calculation, with

9. The growth-accounting equation for computing services is described in the Appendix to this chapter.

the first column showing contributions to gross output and the second column showing contributions to net output.

Contribution to Growth of Gross Output

Starting with real growth rates of inputs—shown in the lower panel— the annual average growth rate of hardware is 17.2 percent, different than the numbers in table 4-1 because the time period is different. For nominal software growth, turn back to table 3-4. The addendum indicates that nominal sales of software increased at an annual rate of 12.6 percent between 1987 and 1993.[10] To convert this to a real growth figure, the 2.7 percent decline in the matched-model deflator for software (shown in the last row of table 3-7) is subtracted, yielding the estimate of real software growth of 9.9 percent a year.[11] Under appropriate assumptions, this real growth rate of sales can be taken as the real growth rate of the stock of software.[12] The figure for growth in computer-related labor is taken directly from table 3-6. As indicated earlier, this employment series does not exactly measure the desired concept, but the rate of change in this type of computer labor likely is a reasonable stand-in for the growth rate of the desired—but unavailable—measure of computer labor.

As for income shares, computer hardware generated about 0.9 percent of total income from 1987 to 1993, on the assumption that computers earned a competitive net return over this period. For software and

10. Oliner and Sichel used the growth in sales of PC Applications software as a proxy for all software sales. Given the broader coverage of software here, it is possible to use the Census Bureau data in table 3-4 that cover a wider segment of the software market. The series cited in the text—with the 12.6 percent growth rate—is based on the data excluding integrated systems after 1990, spliced into the series including integrated systems before 1990. Although it would be preferable to have a series that did not include integrated computer systems for the full time period, the series without integrated systems only starts in 1990. Even so, for the period from 1990 to 1993, when both series with and without integrated systems are available, growth rates are similar, suggesting that the series with integrated systems provides a plausible proxy for the period from 1987 to 1990.

11. As indicated earlier, using the price measure for PC Applications software as a proxy for overall software prices implicitly assumes that prices of non-PC software move similarly to prices of PC Applications software.

12. In particular, a steady-state assumption is necessary for the growth in real sales to equal the growth in the real stock. If software depreciates at a rate δ, the real net stock of software equals a weighted average of past purchases, where the weights equal unity on current period purchases, $1-\delta$ on the previous period, $(1-\delta)^2$ on purchases two periods ago, and so on. In steady state, the growth of the real stock of software equals the growth rate of real purchases.

computer-services labor, Oliner and Sichel used Vijay C. Gurbaxani's estimates of budget shares for hardware, software, and computer-services labor to scale the hardware income share.[13] Scaling the hardware income share in this way implies an income share of 0.7 percent for software and 0.8 percent for computer-services labor.[14]

The top panel of table 4-2 combines figures in the middle and lower panels to show the growth contributions to gross output. These figures reveal that software's contribution to growth is almost as large as that of hardware, while computer-services labor makes an additional modest contribution. When the pieces are added up, the total contribution of computing services to output growth from 1987 to 1993 is 0.31 percentage point a year, about double the contribution of hardware alone. Again, this calculation confirms the importance of broadening the scope beyond hardware alone.

Contribution to Growth of Net Output

As discussed earlier, net output—which strips out the portion of output that covers depreciation costs—is a more appropriate measure of the economy's ability to generate economic well-being than gross output, because the portion of output covering depreciation does not actually make anyone better off.

The second column of table 4-2 shows estimates of the contribution of computing services to net business output between 1987 and 1993. Because net business output excludes depreciation, the growth-accounting equations in chapter 2 must be modified by dropping the depreciation term from the gross return earned by computers. Recall that the gross return, $r_{COMP} + d$, equals the sum of terms for the competitive return and for depreciation. To calculate a contribution to net output, the term for depreciation is dropped in the calculation of income shares.[15]

---

13. Gurbaxani (1990).

14. The hardware income share is 0.9 percent. As already discussed, Gurbaxani's budget shares indicate that software purchases were 74 percent of hardware spending, while outlays for computer-services labor and other inputs were 89 percent of hardware spending. Scaling by these shares implies the software income share of 0.7 percent ($= 0.74 \times 0.9$) and the computer-services labor income share of 0.8 percent ($= 0.89 \times 0.9$).

15. One other modification must be made to the growth-accounting expressions in chapter 2—to get a contribution to net output. Namely, changing the nominal output measure appearing in the denominator of the income share to a net output measure. The calculations reported here use net domestic product for nonfarm business less housing. This output figure is reported in table 1-12 of the National Income and Product Accounts.

For computer hardware, table 4-2 shows that the net income share for computer hardware is just 0.3 percent, only about one-third of the gross income share. This drop in the income share occurs because costs of obsolescence (depreciation) account for about two-thirds of the neoclassical gross return to computers. With this lower income share, the contribution of hardware to growth in net output falls to 0.06 percentage point a year, less than a tenth of a percentage point a year.

For computer software, the net income share is calculated by scaling the gross income share to net out depreciation and to account for the smaller size of total net income compared with total gross income. This adjustment yields a net income share for software of 0.3 percent, notably lower than the gross share.[16] With this lower share, the contribution of software to growth in net output averages to just 0.04 percentage point a year. For computer-services labor, the income share is unaffected by depreciation but is boosted slightly by other adjustments.[17]

When the pieces are added up, the top line of the table shows that the contribution of computing services to net output growth was 0.15 percentage point a year between 1987 and 1993. This figure is much smaller than the analogous gross contributions because depreciation accounts for such a large share of the gross return to computer hardware and software. Thus, from a welfare point of view, computing services made a modest contribution over this period, on the assumption that computers were as productive at the firm level as any other type of capital.

16. Recall that the gross income share of software—estimated at 0.7 percent—can be expressed as the gross return, $r_{COMP} + d$, multiplied by the nominal stock of software divided by total nominal gross output. To calculate a net income share with depreciation removed, the gross return must be replaced by the net return, r_{COMP}, and gross output must be replaced by net output. To make these adjustments, the gross income share for software is multiplied by $r_{COMP}/(r_{COMP} + d)$ and by (gross output/net output). For these calculations, r_{COMP} is set at 12.1 percent and d at 25 percent, implying that the gross income share must be multiplied by 0.326. For the second adjustment, the gross output to net output ratio for 1993 is 1.12, using gross and net figures for nonfarm business output less housing from tables 1-7 and 1-12 in the National Income and Product Accounts. Thus, the net income share for software is 0.26 (= 0.326 × 1.12 × 0.7).

17. The gross income share of computer-services labor averaged 0.8 percent between 1987 and 1993. In 1993 the ratio of gross income to net income was 1.12, with data for gross and net nonfarm business product less housing from tables 1-7 and 1-12 of the National Income and Product Accounts. Thus, the net income share of computer-services labor is 0.9 (= 1.12 × 0.8).

Consumer Surplus

Earlier it was mentioned that consumer surplus provides a further benefit to society from declining computer prices that is not captured by estimates in the previous section. Namely, as the price of computers continues to fall, those who would have purchased computers even at the old, higher prices receive a bonus because they need no longer pay that higher price. Consumer surplus is difficult to measure with precision, although some authors have provided rough estimates. For example, Ken Flamm estimated that consumer surplus would boost the income flow from computer hardware by 20 to 40 percent.[18] While important, such estimates can not simply be added directly to those in table 4-2 because consumer surplus is not included in measures of output growth. A full accounting of consumer surplus's role in economic welfare—including consumer surplus accruing from all goods and services in the economy—is well beyond the scope of this study.

Neoclassical Growth Contributions and the Productivity Slowdown

Table 4-2 shows that the neoclassical contribution of computers to growth in gross output is 0.31 percentage point a year, while the contribution to growth in net output is about half as much. Are these contributions large or small? Viewed from one perspective, they are rather small, amounting to only a few tenths of a percentage point. Moreover, they are quite small compared with the size of the productivity slowdown of the early 1970s. At that time, productivity growth slowed by about one and one-half percentage points. In comparison to that slowdown, the contributions of computing services in recent years remains small, suggesting that computers have been too small a factor to have reversed that decline, at least on the neoclassical assumption that computer hardware and software earn a competitive return.

Viewed from another perspective, these contributions are more significant. For growth in gross output, the annual contribution of 0.31 percentage point accounts for a sizable fraction of overall growth. In fact,

---

18. Flamm (1987, pp. 32–35). Flamm's upper-bound estimate is based on a calculation in which computer prices fall at an annual rate of 30 percent. BEA's price measure for computer and peripheral equipment suggests declines of a smaller magnitude in the 1970s and 1980s, which would lower the amount of consumer surplus generated.

with overall growth in gross output averaging just 2.0 percent a year from 1987 to 1993, computing services were responsible for one-sixth of that overall growth, on the assumption that computer hardware and software earned a competitive net return. Thus, even though computer hardware and software make up a relatively small share of the nation's capital stock, they still have accounted for a sizable share of all economic growth. Moreover, when viewed in terms of productivity growth, this comparison is more dramatic. As shown in figure 1-4, growth in labor productivity has averaged about 1.1 percent since the early 1970s and increased at an annual rate of 0.9 percent between 1987 and 1993. Over this period, computer hardware and software together contributed about one-quarter percentage point a year to growth in labor productivity from 1987 to 1993, implying that computer hardware and software accounted for more than one-fourth of the overall growth in productivity.[19]

What About Supernormal Returns?

The previous section demonstrated that the neoclassical contribution of computing services to the growth of output has been modest compared with the size of the early 1970s productivity slowdown. Many would argue, however, that the neoclassical contribution misses much of the impact of computers. As discussed in chapter 2, computer technology may enable firms to exploit new profit opportunities and to earn a supernormal return. To the extent that computers do earn supernormal returns, the neoclassical analysis in the last section would understate their contribution to growth.[20]

How big could these supernormal returns to computers plausibly be? Oliner and Sichel examined this question by recalculating the contribution of computers to growth allowing for supernormal returns of a magnitude estimated in recent studies.[21] The two studies generating the highest estimates of returns are discussed here.

Erik Brynjolfsson and Lorin Hitt estimated the return earned on computer hardware at 367 large firms between 1987 and 1991.[22] As Oliner

19. Labor productivity is defined as output per hour. In table 4-2 only computer hardware and software contribute directly to labor productivity; additional output growth arising from increases in computer-services labor would not boost labor productivity.
20. This section draws heavily on Oliner and Sichel (1994, especially pages 288–93).
21. Oliner and Sichel (1994).
22. See Erik Brynjolfsson and Lorin Hitt, "Paradox Lost? Firm-Level Information on

and Sichel describe, Brynjolfsson and Hitt report a gross annual return to computer hardware of 81 percent, well above the neoclassical estimate of the gross return of about 37 percent. To get a figure for the return net of depreciation, subtract Oliner and Sichel's estimate of depreciation and obsolescence charges of 25 percent from Brynjolfsson and Hitt's figure. This subtraction implies a net nominal return of 56 percent (= 81 − 25), several times higher than the competitive net return of 12 percent implicit in the neoclassical setup.

The estimate in Brynjolfsson and Hitt raises the possibility that computers earn supernormal returns and therefore make a larger contribution to output growth than implied by the neoclassical view. But how plausible is such a large rate of return? In broad terms, there are three reasons to be skeptical that returns could be as large as implied by this study. First, although Brynjolfsson and Hitt's point estimate is quite large, so too are the associated standard errors, suggesting that substantial uncertainty surrounds the estimated rate of return.[23]

Second, Brynjolfsson and Hitt's rate of return is calculated without regard for software, the omission of which could bias upward their estimated rate of return.[24] Brynjolfsson and Hitt's procedure estimates the ratio of the income flow from computer hardware to total income and backs out the implied rate of return, given data on the stock of computers and total income. Because software is not included in their econometric equation, the estimated income flow to hardware may be overstated because part of the income flow that actually should be attributed to software may be attributed to hardware. To the extent that the income

---

the Returns to Information Systems Spending," *Management Science*, vol. 42 (April 1996), pp. 541–58. These authors use firm-level data from an annual survey conducted by the International Data Corporation (IDC), covering 1987–91. The 367 firms included in the survey accounted for a sizable share of the U.S. business sector, generating sales of nearly $2 trillion in 1991. Frank Lichtenberg (1993) also analyzed firm-level returns to computers and obtained similar results.

23. A 95 percent confidence interval around Brynjolfsson and Hitt's gross return estimate of 81 percent nearly encompasses Oliner and Sichel's neoclassical estimate of 37 percent.

24. Econometrically, their estimating equation is subject to omitted variable bias. They regress output growth on terms for the growth in computer hardware and other capital and in computer-related and other labor. In their framework, the rate of return on computer hardware can be backed out from the estimated coefficient on growth in computer hardware; the larger is this estimated coefficient, the larger is the implied rate of return to computer hardware. By omitting software from their equation, however, the coefficient on hardware probably would be biased upward if the growth in computer hardware is correlated with the growth in software. Because growth rates for hardware and software are probably highly correlated, it is quite plausible that their implied rate of return is overstated.

flow to hardware is overstated, the rate of return implied by their equation would be too high. Consider the case in which all of the income flow from software were incorrectly attributed to hardware by their estimation procedure. In this case, the income shares in table 4-2 imply that the income flow from hardware was overstated by a factor of about 1.8.[25] If their procedure overstated the income flow to hardware by a factor of 1.8, it would overstate the rate of return by the same factor. Thus, if Brynjolfsson and Hitt's 81 percent return were overstated by a factor of 1.8, the actual gross return would be about 46 percent [= (81 percent)/ 1.8)], not that far above the neoclassical estimate of 37 percent. Brynjolfsson and Hitt are aware of this difficulty. They consider an example in which omitted factors—such as software—cut in half their estimated rate of return of 81 percent, which would put their return remarkably close to Oliner and Sichel's estimate of the neoclassical rate of return.

A third reason to be skeptical about large estimated rates of return is that such returns would imply that, at least ex post facto, many businesses behaved irrationally. If businesses knew that large excess returns to computers were available—and so much larger than other available investments and the firms' cost of capital—then companies should have invested even more heavily in computing equipment than they did. That is, the availability of supernormal returns implies that—at least after the fact—many companies underinvested in computers.

Is such underinvestment plausible? Brynjolfsson and Hitt's sample focused on large companies.[26] Most of these companies would already have been using computers for many years and would have been broadly familiar with the technology, raising questions about the argument that excess returns are earned on computers because they are such a new technology. Moreover, most of these large companies would have had easy access to credit markets, suggesting that they would not have faced constraints in financing additional purchases of computing services were such additional investment desired. Finally, the interview evidence described in box 4-1 suggests that most of the interviewed companies were not earning supernormal returns on computers, although such anecdotal evidence must be interpreted very cautiously.

25. The factor of 1.8 is calculated from the income shares in table 4-2, as the ratio of the total gross income share for hardware and software to the income share for hardware alone [1.8 = (0.9 + 0.7)/0.9].

26. Their sample drew from Fortune 500 manufacturing and Fortune 500 service firms. Brynjolfsson and Hitt (1996).

Box 4-1. *Supernormal Returns*

Companies were asked in the focused interviews whether, given extra resources, they would devote them to information technology or to other aspects of the business. If information technology were earning a better return than other investments and the firm's cost of capital, then the extra resources should be devoted to information technology because the highest return would be earned there. However, if companies would not devote extra resources to information technology, then—at least on the marginal dollar—these companies are not earning supernormal returns on their information technology investments.

Most respondents indicated that extra resources would not be put into information technology because about as much as possible was being done on that front. Among the smaller companies interviewed, Bill Lake, comanaging partner at the law firm Wilmer, Cutler, and Pickering put it, "If we had an additional $2 million, would we put it into technology? I don't think so, but that's because we're already committed to buying what we need to fit our philosophy." The other law firm, Hale and Dorr, and the engineering consulting firm indicated they would devote additional resources to bringing new expertise into the firm. As put by Don Ross, CEO of the engineering firm, "If we had any extra funds, my first commitment would be to hire somebody we really wanted to get."

Only one of the larger mainframe-using companies indicated a clear desire to put additional resources into technology. Among the other large companies that were not inclined to put the additional resources into information technology, a typical responses was, "Historically, we've had a serious commitment to technology. Even though I work in Information Systems, I think the real gain for the business will come from [expanding the business in other ways.]" A slightly more shaded response was, "If I simply said, I have $5 million more dollars, could I spend it on Information Services, the answer is absolutely yes. The harder question is whether I could get better value by putting it somewhere else. It's not so simple as to say that it would go to Information Services."

One last quote perhaps best summarizes the general view expressed, that investment in information technology by these companies is proceeding at about the right pace: "[Last year, we put additional resources into technology. Right now,] we're doing what we think we have to do to maintain competitive advantage and we're doing as much as we think we can digest."

With these caveats in mind, how large a contribution is implied by Brynjolfsson and Hitt's estimate of the rate of return? Their estimated gross return of 81 percent implies a net return of 56 percent, which is more than four times larger than the neoclassical return of 12 percent. If these returns are assumed to apply to software as well as to hardware, then from 1987 to 1993 the yearly contribution of computing services to gross output would have been 0.62 percentage point and the contribution to growth in net output would be 0.51 percentage point.[27] These contributions are well above those shown in table 4-2; however, they are still notably smaller than the one and one-half percentage point slowdown in productivity growth in the early 1970s. Moreover, the growth contributions implied by Brynjolfsson and Hitt's work would be notably lower if their rate of return were adjusted downward to take account of software in the way suggested above. As indicated, such an adjustment could imply a gross rate of return quite close to the neoclassical return of 37 percent.[28]

In another often-cited and interesting study, Alan Krueger provided evidence that individuals who use computers at work receive a 10 to 15 percent wage premium relative to other workers.[29] Oliner and Sichel use this number, other figures from Krueger's paper, and one key assumption to calculate the rate of return and growth contribution of computer hardware. The key assumption is that the wage premium reflects an increase in the wages and productivity of those who use computers at

27. To obtain the contribution to gross output growth with Brynjolfsson and Hitt's 81 percent return, the contributions of computer hardware and software in table 4-2 are raised by a factor of 2.19 [= 81/37], yielding a contribution of 0.57 percentage point. Adding in the computer labor contribution of 0.05 percentage point from table 4-2—which is not affected by the rate of return to capital—yields an overall contribution of computing services to output growth of 0.62 percentage point. For net output with a 56 percent net return, the net contributions of computer hardware and software in table 4.2 are raised by a factor of 4.67 [= 56/12], yielding a contribution of 0.46 percentage point. Adding in the computer labor contribution of 0.05 percentage point from table 4-2 yields an overall contribution of computing services to net output growth of 0.51 percentage point.

28. The 46 percent gross return calculated in the text by scaling back Brynjolfsson and Hitt's return to take account of software would imply a yearly growth contribution of 0.37 percentage point, only slightly above the neoclassical contribution of 0.31 percentage point. To obtain the 0.37 percentage point figure, the gross contributions of computer hardware and software in table 4-2 are raised by a factor of 1.23 [= 45.5/37.1], yielding a contribution of 0.32 percentage point. Adding in the computer labor contribution of 0.05 percentage point from table 4-2 yields the 0.37 percentage point figure.

29. Krueger (1993, p. 35). DiNardo and Pischke (1996) argue that Krueger's results reflect unobserved heterogeneity of workers, rather than a true productivity effect of the use of computers at work.

work, rather than a decline in the wages and productivity of those who do not use computers. On that assumption, they translated Krueger's wage premium into a rate of return on computer hardware of 68.2 percent, but like Brynjolfsson and Hitt, Oliner and Sichel did not take account of software in translating Krueger's estimates to a rate of return.[30] Just as in that earlier discussion, however, taking account of software would scale down this return by a factor of 1.8, implying a gross rate of return of about 38 percent. Such a rate of return is barely above the estimated neoclassical gross return of 37 percent. Thus it appears that Krueger's results on the computer-wage premium are broadly consistent with the neoclassical growth-accounting results.

A final point about the arithmetic of returns and contributions to growth in gross output should be noted. Recall that the contribution to growth depends on the neoclassical gross return of 37 percent, which consists of a net return of about 12 percent and a depreciation charge of about 25 percent. Suppose that the net return of 12 percent doubles to 24 percent. In this example, the gross return would rise to 49 percent (the sum of the 24 percent net return and the 25 percent depreciation charge), which represents only about a one-third increase from 37 percent. Thus a doubling of the net return only boosts the gross return by about one-third. This arithmetic arises because the net return only accounts for about one-third of the gross return to computers. So even if computer hardware and software earn net returns that are much higher than neoclassical net returns, the arithmetic here limits the degree to which such excess returns could boost contributions to growth of gross output.

Mismeasurement of Output

Many commentators have pointed out that information technology produces output that is intangible and difficult to measure.[31] And, as dis-

---

30. Oliner and Sichel actually report that a rate of return slightly different than 68.2 percent is consistent with Krueger's results. The discrepancy reflects the correction of a minor programming error.

31. Although undermeasurement of real output growth could reflect missing nominal output, most research has focused on problems with the price indexes used to translate nominal output to real output. Further, much of this research has focused on inadequate adjustments for quality changes—especially in services—and on late introduction of new products into the samples used for price indexes.

cussed in box 4-2, the company interviews confirmed the difficulty of measuring the benefits generated by computers and calculating rates of return on these investments. Given these measurement difficulties, some analysts have suggested that part of the resolution of the computer productivity paradox lies in measurement issues; as described in chapter 2, this argument suggests that if only better tools were available for measuring the economy, the contribution of computers to output growth would be more evident.[32] This section explores this conjecture and argues that mismeasurement of output can probably explain only a small part of the computer paradox or the productivity slowdown.

Mismeasurement and Neoclassical Contributions to Growth

Many studies—such as the research by Brynjolfsson and Hitt—use data on real output and the stock of computers to estimate a rate of return. For those studies, unmeasured output generated by computers would imply that the estimated rate of return was lower than the actual rate of return. In contrast, output mismeasurement would have little effect on the neoclassical contributions to growth described earlier in the chapter. To see this, recall that the estimates of computing services' contribution to output growth were derived from the input side *and do not rely on estimates of real output growth.*[33] That is, the neoclassical contribution to output is calculated from the capital and labor inputs that generate computing services, along with assumed rates of return for these inputs. Thus mismeasurement of output would not affect *neoclassical* contributions to growth.

But suppose one wanted to assert that—because of mismeasurement of output growth—actual contributions to growth were significantly larger than the neoclassical estimates. Taking the data on stocks of hardware and software as given, the only way that the contribution of com-

32. For example, see Baily and Quinn (1994); National Research Council (1994); Griliches (1994); and Brynjolfsson (1993).

33. Nominal output does enter this calculation, but as indicated earlier, most researchers have assumed that nominal output is reasonably well measured and that the problems lie in the price indexes used to translate nominal output to real output. Mismeasurement of the computer capital stock or of labor inputs to computing services could, of course, affect the estimated contributions. For example, if computer prices have fallen more rapidly than estimated by the BEA—as suggested by Berndt, Griliches, and Rappaport (1990)—then the correct contribution of computing services to output growth would be larger than calculated above. But most discussions of the computer paradox focus on the difficulty of measuring the intangible output produced by computers.

Box 4-2. *The Difficulty of Quantitatively Measuring Rates of Return to Information Technology*

In the interviews, many questions were asked about the payoffs and productivity impacts of information technology. These questions always elicited qualitative answers that emphasized the intangible nature of the benefits of information technology and the difficulty of capturing these benefits in return-on-investment calculations. Thus, in making decisions about information technology, these companies often rely on qualitative or judgmental criteria.

Among the smaller companies, the law firms emphasized that computer technology improved quality and accuracy, enhanced flexibility, and allowed them to get more work done in a given amount of time. Measurement, however, is difficult. Michael Klein, a managing partner at Wilmer, Cutler, and Pickering, stated flatly, "I don't know how to measure the productivity of lawyers." John Hamilton, the managing partner at Hale and Dorr, summarized the issue this way, "I think [these investments in information technology] have paid big dividends, but I can't sit here and quantify them for you. We haven't done that kind of cost analysis. We know intuitively that we're able to deliver a better product faster, and we've done well so it's worked." Maurice Garoutte, senior systems analyst at the engineering firm said, "I'd like to say we do rigorous cost-benefit analysis [of these investments], but that would not be the truth."

The larger firms relying on mainframe power as well as desktop equipment appear to go further in evaluating prospective technology projects with quantitative tools, but sometimes this kind of measurement just cannot be accomplished. A respondent at one of the larger companies summarized this view as:

> Every investment in technology has its payback, and we take a disciplined approach. We look at each investment and ask if it will either increase service to our clients or lower costs. . . . Sometimes paybacks can be quantified financially; in other cases paybacks [are hard to quantify] and come about by increasing value to our clients in the form of service. It's not a science, it's an art.

St. Paul's Senior Vice President for Information Systems Wayne Hoeschen said, "We do the standard sort of financial analysis everyone does, but we don't let that make the decision for us."

puting services could be considerably higher than the neoclassical estimate is if actual returns exceed the assumed neoclassical return. Thus an assertion that the neoclassical contribution to output growth is too low because some of the output generated by computers is not measured is essentially an assertion that computer hardware and software earn supernormal returns. While it is possible that these inputs have earned supernormal returns, the arguments of the last section raise questions about how likely this is to have occurred. Thus unless one is prepared to assert that computer hardware or software earned supernormal returns, mismeasurement of output growth will have little impact on the size of the neoclassical contribution of computing services to output growth.

A Broader Perspective

The last section showed that mismeasurement of real output alone would have little impact on the neoclassical contributions to output growth, unless it were assumed that the inputs to computing services generated supernormal returns. But there is another question that goes beyond the neoclassical contribution of computing services to output growth. Namely, why has the growth of output and productivity been so sluggish in the past two decades if the nation is in the midst of a technological revolution?

Measurement error is often suggested as a resolution of this broader puzzle, and the recent Boskin Commission report on mismeasurement in the Consumer Price Index (CPI) has brought welcome attention to these issues recently. A simple equation, however, highlights two factors that place limits on the degree to which mismeasurement of real output could explain the computer productivity paradox or the productivity slowdown of the 1970s. Let

(4-3)   (true output growth) = (measured output growth)

+ (measurement gap).

In equation 4-3, a big measurement gap implies that measured output growth is less than true output growth. Here is one aspect of the measurement error story as often told.[34] Manufactured goods are easier to measure than services or information-based products. Moreover, in the

---

34. See Michael J. Mandel, "The Real Truth about the Economy," *Business Week*, November 7, 1994, pp. 110–18; and Griliches (1994).

1950s and 1960s, manufactured goods constituted a bigger share of the economy than today. Thus the measurement gap in equation 4-3 was relatively small in the 1950s and 1960s, when output and productivity growth were robust. As intangible services became more important in the 1970s and 1980s—including those produced by a host of new information technologies—the measurement gap in equation 4-3 rose, pushing measured output growth below actual output growth. On its face, this explanation sounds plausible. But a deeper look raises two further issues: the degree to which measurement error affects final demand rather than just leading to a reshuffling of output among industries and the degree to which measurement error has increased over time.[35]

Measurement Error and Final Demand

To avoid double counting, gross domestic product (GDP) only adds up components of final demand—that is, purchases of goods and services by their final user.[36] For example, purchases of goods and services by households count as final demand, but purchases of materials or services by businesses do not count as final demand because these materials will be transformed into products that will be resold. Because GDP is constructed this way, mismeasurement of some type of output can only affect the overall measurement gap for real GDP if the mismeasured item is a component of final demand; if mismeasurement affects an intermediate input that is not a part of final demand, then that mismeasurement would merely imply a reshuffling of output across industries. And the final-demand share of many services associated with information technology—such as financial services—is relatively small.

Consider the example of financial services, an area that has been heavily affected by information technology. The financial services purchased by a manufacturer of household appliances are not counted di-

35. Both of these issues were raised forcefully by Baily and Gordon (1988) and by Gordon (1996).

36. In terms of GDP, final demand consists of the product-side components of GDP, including purchases of goods and services by households, purchases of equipment, structures, and inventories by businesses, purchases of goods and services by the government, and purchases by foreigners of goods and services produced in the United States less purchases by those in the United States of goods and services produced in other countries. In the nomenclature of national income accounting, these components of final demand are described by the well-known identity that $Y = C + I + G + (X - M)$, where Y is GDP, C is consumption, I is investment by businesses in equipment, structures, and inventories, G is government purchases, and $X - M$ is net exports of goods and services.

rectly in GDP, but rather get into GDP implicitly because they contribute to the value of the appliances produced by the manufacturer. If the financial services purchased by this appliance maker were added separately into GDP along with the full value of the appliances produced, GDP would incorrectly double count the value of these financial services. Thus mismeasurement of financial services would lead to mismeasurement of real GDP only to the extent that financial services are part of final demand. And because business purchases of financial services are not part of final demand, household purchases of financial services are the primary way that financial services get into final demand.

Now consider the portion of financial services' output that is not counted as final demand. What are the implications of mismeasurement of this portion for industry output? Once a measure of GDP is obtained by adding up final purchases of goods and services, the Commerce Department allocates this GDP among industries to obtain measures of output by industry. If the output of the financial services industry were undermeasured, then the inputs of financial services purchased by other industries—say, the appliance maker—would necessarily be understated. Since industry value added is the total value of output less the value of inputs, an understatement of the value of purchased financial services by a producer of household appliances would lead to an overstatement of value added in the appliance industry. Thus—except for the portion of financial services that gets into final demand—the undermeasurement of financial services would only lead to a reshuffling of output from the financial services industry to those industries purchasing these services, such as the appliance industry. While such reshuffling of output across industries would have important implications for understanding productivity performance within industries, this reshuffling would not affect the aggregate measurement gap in equation 4-3 and could not explain the recent sluggishness in productivity growth.[37]

These points can be made more concrete by putting some numbers on the example of financial services, a sector widely believed to be subject to mismeasurement. Financial services often are defined to include the finance, insurance, and real estate industries. The value of total output produced by these industries accounted for 9.6 percent of nominal GDP in 1994.[38] But a significant portion of this output was sold to other

37. Owing to this difficulty of allocating output across industries, measurement problems at the industry or sector level are thought by many to be severe. For example, see Baily and Gordon (1988); and Denison (1989).

38. See Yuskavage (1996). For the figure in the text, the output of the finance and

companies as intermediate input and did not count as final demand. As a share of final demand, financial services purchased by consumers accounted for just 4.6 percent of GDP in 1994, less than half of the total output produced by this indusry.[39] Thus, even if computers have generated a difficult-to-measure explosion in the quality and variety of financial services, this undermeasurement could only have a modest effect on the measurement gap in equation 4-3 because the final demand share of financial services is modest.

Has Measurement Error Increased over Time?

The second critical issue highlighted by equation 4-3 is that the crux of the measurement error explanation is an *increase* in the measurement gap in the past two decades because the puzzle is a *decrease* in output growth over that period. To see why a rise in the measurement gap is the key to this story, suppose that the measurement gap has always been 1 percentage point; that is, output growth has always been undermeasured by 1 percentage point. Then—as equation 4-3 makes clear—the drop-off in measured output growth experienced in the 1970s and 1980s must correspond to a drop-off in true output growth, because the amount of undermeasurement would have been the same before and after the growth slowdown. Thus a measurement gap can explain a slowdown in measured output growth compared with the 1950s and 1960s only if the measurement gap has increased to push measured output growth further below actual output growth. As described by the Boskin Commission, and as Robert Gordon has discussed elsewhere, many factors probably contribute to a sizable measurement gap.[40] But, unless these factors led to an increase in the measurement gap, stories about mismeasurement of output provide no help in understanding the slowdown of economic growth in the past two decades.

---

insurance industries is calculated as the output of the finance, insurance, and real estate industry less nonfarm housing services; this total equals $668.5 billion. Total GDP is $6931.4 billion.

39. See National Income and Product Account tables in *Survey of Current Business*, vol. 76 (August 1996), pp. 30, 49, tables 2-4, 5-6. Purchases of finance, insurance, and real estate services by consumers are calculated as the sum of brokers' commissions on the sale of residential structures from table 5-6 plus the following items from table 2-4: brokerage charges, bank service charges, services furnished without payment, and the expense of handling life insurance. Altogether, these items add up to $317.6 billion in 1994.

40. Gordon (1996).

Has the measurement gap risen dramatically in the past two decades? This is a very difficult question; just estimating the size of the measurement gap for GDP growth is tough enough, let alone trying to determine how this measurement gap has changed over time. Nevertheless, three types of evidence suggest that the measurement gap may not have opened up enough to explain the computer paradox of the 1980s or the productivity slowdown of the 1970s.[41]

First, mismeasurement of output growth is not a new phenomenon resulting just from recent technological innovations or structural changes in the economy. Thirty-six years ago, in 1961, the Stigler Committee identified several problems contributing to a worrisome measurement gap at that time, including slow introduction of new products into price index samples and inadequate adjustment for quality change.[42] Of course, in 1961 the Stigler Committee was not concerned with computers but rather with relatively new products that were in the nexus of innovation at that time, including televisions, synthetic fabrics, and medical drugs. More recently, the Boskin Commission has provided evidence that a substantial measurement gap persists. That report, however, did not argue that the measurement gap has increased significantly over time.[43] Perhaps the measurement gap associated with products that were undergoing rapid change in the 1950s and 1960s has been replaced by a measurement gap associated with newer products, which are in the nexus of innovation today. And if the measurement gap today is the same size as in the early 1960s, mismeasurement can not explain the sluggish pace of economic growth over the past two decades.[44]

41. One factor that has led to an increase in the measurement gap is a methodological change in the Consumer Price Index (CPI) implemented in 1978. At that time, the U.S. Dept. of Labor, Bureau of Labor Statistics (BLS), changed its procedures for calculating the CPI in a way that introduced what has come to be known as "formula bias." BLS identified the problem and recently took steps to eliminate formula bias. Based on simulation results, BLS suggested that this bias caused the CPI to overstate inflation by 0.2 to 0.25 percentage point before its correction. (See U.S. Department of Labor (1996, pp. 4–5). Because consumption is roughly two-thirds of GDP, this overstatement of inflation in the CPI would have caused real GDP growth to be understated between 0.1 and 0.2 percentage point.

42. NBER (1961, pp. 23–49).

43. The Boskin Commission report does suggest that the bias in the CPI from quality change increased by a little more than 0.1 percentage point a year between 1980 and 1996 (p. 63).

44. Moreover, since the Stigler report called attention to the measurement problem, economists and government statistical agencies have made substantial progress in improving official economic statistics.

Reinforcing the idea that measurement error has been a problem for a long time, William Nordhaus constructed a price index for lighting back to the beginning of the nineteenth century.[45] He found that conventional measures of lighting overstated price growth by a dramatic amount, implying that output growth was substantially understated going back to the Industrial Revolution. Again, mismeasurement has been with us for a very long time.

The second type of evidence weighing in against a rapidly growing measurement gap consists of a couple of recent studies that have looked explicitly at whether measurement error has worsened over time; these studies concluded that the measurement gap probably has not grown much. Donald Siegel examined measurement error in the producer price index (PPI), comparing the amount of mismeasurement between 1972 and 1977 to the amount of mismeasurement between 1977 and 1982.[46] He found that the PPI significantly overstates inflation in both periods, but by roughly the same amount. According to this study, "Mismeasurement of output prices is constant over time, implying that errors of measurement are not a significant determinant of either the slowdown or recent acceleration in manufacturing productivity."[47] Although the scope of this research study is limited—focusing on a relatively short time period and on just the manufacturing sector of the economy—it provides some evidence against the hypothesis of a growing measurement gap.

In another study, Martin Neil Baily and Robert Gordon did a detailed analysis of mismeasurement in many parts of the economy, focusing especially on services.[48] They found compelling evidence that some components of output, including business and financial services and airline travel, are substantially undermeasured and that the amount of under-measurement likely has grown over time. Nevertheless, the share of these components in the economy was small enough that worsening mismeasurement for these items had little impact on the measurement gap for the economy as a whole.

The third type of evidence against a growing measurement gap undercuts the argument that a rising services share has significantly boosted the measurement gap. To recap, that argument is that the continuing *shift* in economic activity toward the service sector, where output growth

45. Nordhaus (1994).
46. Siegel (1994).
47. Siegel (1994, p. 11).
48. Baily and Gordon (1988).

may be substantially undermeasured, has significantly boosted the measurement gap for the economy as a whole.

In a recent paper, I assessed this argument and concluded that it is of limited quantitative significance.[49] That paper showed that the increase in the measurement gap from a rising service share depends on the size of the shift toward the service sector and on how much worse the measurement of output growth is in the service-producing sector than in the goods-producing sector. In particular, the boost to the overall measurement gap from a rising services share equals the increase in the share of services multiplied by how much more the growth in services is undermeasured than the growth in goods is undermeasured. Although estimating the pieces of this relationship is difficult, a rough order of magnitude can be obtained.

In that paper, I demonstrated that even when the measure that gives the biggest increase in the services share of output is used, the increase in that share from the period before 1972 to the period after 1980 is less than ten percentage points.[50] And based on two detailed studies of mismeasurement, I concluded that an upper bound on the relative measurement gap between services and goods is two and one-half percentage points.[51] Multiplying these two figures together to obtain the impact of a rising service share on the overall measurement gap implies a boost to the overall measurement gap of about one-quarter percentage point. Such a figure is much less than the 1.5 percentage point slowdown in growth in the early 1970s and suggests that the interaction of mismeasurement and a higher services share is an unlikely explanation for the sluggish pace of output and productivity growth in the past two decades.

One final challenge should be issued to those who argue that measurement error can explain the poor performance of the U.S. economy in the past two decades. If the slowdown in output growth in recent decades has really only reflected an increase in measurement error, then why have so many people in the United States recently expressed concern

49. See Daniel Sichel, "The Productivity Slowdown: Is a Growing Unmeasurable Sector the Culprit?" *Review of Economics and Statistics,* forthcoming.

50. This figure is based on nominal shares of output on an industry basis. The services share corresponds to the "unmeasurable" sector in Griliches (1994), which includes construction and excludes transportation and public utility services. The goods sector corresponds to Griliches's "measurable" sector, which includes everything else. On this measure, the average share of services from 1950 to 1972 is 56.2 percent, and from 1980 to 1990 the average share is 65.6 percent. These figures yield a 9.4 percentage point increase in the service share.

51. These two studies are Popkin (1992); and Lebow, Roberts, and Stockton (1992).

about economic insecurity and dissatisfaction with the economy's performance?

Looking Ahead

Thus far, this chapter has shown that computing services' contribution to growth is modest compared with the size of the productivity slowdown of the 1970s, provided that computer hardware and software earn a competitive rate of return. But that analysis only extends through the early 1990s. What about the future? Could the nation be on the cusp of a computer-driven productivity surge? For example, Paul David has suggested that a long lag ensues before the productivity benefits of new technologies like computers become apparent.[52] This section uses the analytic framework of chapter 2 to examine future possibilities.[53] The main message is that even with very rapid growth of hardware, software, and labor inputs, the contribution of computing services to growth is not likely to rise substantially in coming years unless the rate of return earned by computer hardware and software were to surge upward. Although such an outcome is possible, there are reasons to discount its likelihood.

Three Scenarios for the Future

Predicting the future is highly perilous, and what follows should be taken as only suggestive. Having said that, Oliner and Sichel extended the growth-accounting framework to the future and an adaptation of their work is reported here.[54] They projected the contribution to growth of computing services—the joint product of hardware, software, and labor inputs associated with computers—through 2003 under several scenarios. They start with three scenarios—pessimistic, midrange, and optimistic—in which hardware and software earn the same competitive net return generated by other capital. Later, the possibility of a takeoff in the returns earned by hardware and software is considered.

52. David (1989, 1990).
53. Much of the material in this section is taken directly from Oliner and Sichel (1994, pp. 306–13). Figures for the hardware and labor components here differ slightly from those in Oliner and Sichel owing to the correction of a minor programming error. Figures for software differ because the software figures used here cover a broader segment of the software market than the figures in Oliner and Sichel, which were based on PC Applications software.
54. Oliner and Sichel (1994, pp. 307–09).

Table 4-3. *Projected Contributions of Computing Services to Growth in Gross Output*[a]

Item	1993 actual	2003			
		Pessimistic	Midrange	Optimistic	Takeoff
Contributions from[b]					
Computing services[c]	.34	.21	.34	.50	.64
Hardware	.20	.11	.18	.27	.35
Software	.08	.07	.11	.16	.21
Computer-services labor	.06	.03	.05	.07	.07
Income shares[d]					
Computing services[c]	2.2	1.7	2.3	2.8	3.5
Hardware	.8	.6	.9	1.1	1.5
Software	.6	.5	.6	.8	1.1
Computer-services labor	.7	.6	.8	1.0	1.0

Source: Methodology from Oliner and Sichel (1994). Figures differ from theirs for several reasons. For hardware and labor, differences reflect the correction of a minor programming error. Figures for software differ because the growth rates for nominal software cover a broader segment of the software market than the figures in Oliner and Sichel. Finally, the take-off scenario presented here uses a different rate of return assumption than in Oliner and Sichel.

a. Computing services include computer hardware (CPE), software, and computer-services labor.
b. Percentage point a year.
c. Components may not sum to total because of rounding.
d. Percent.

For the pessimistic scenario, the stock of computers is assumed to grow at its average rate over the years 1988–93, which includes the 1990–91 recession. In this scenario, the real stock of computers and peripheral equipment (CPE) grows at about 17 percent. The midrange scenario, based on average growth rates over the nine years from 1984 to 1993, posits that the real stock of CPE increases at more than 20 percent a year. Finally, the optimistic scenario—based on the robust growth rates of 1993—assumes that this stock rises at an annual rate exceeding 24 percent.[55] Details on the scenarios are shown in the Appendix to this chapter, in table 4A-1.

Starting with gross output, projections of the growth contribution under each scenario are shown in table 4-3 and figure 4-2. As can be seen in that table and figure, the midrange scenario yields a contribution of computing services to output growth in 2003 of 0.34 percentage point, the same as in 1993. Under the optimistic scenario, the contribution of computing services rises, but not especially rapidly, moving up to 0.50 percentage point by 2003. Under the pessimistic scenario, the gross contribution to growth falls to 0.21 percentage point.

55. Remember, these projections are working off the real stock of computing equipment, not the yearly flow of new investment. In a given year, the growth in real investment can far exceed the growth in the real capital stock.

Figure 4-2. *Growth Contributions of Computing Services to Gross Output*

Percentage points

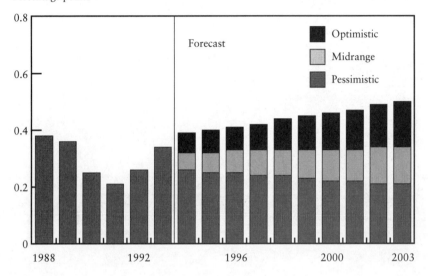

Source: Methodology from Oliner and Sichel (1994). Figures differ from theirs, reflecting a different series for software and the correction of a minor programming error.

Table 4-4. *Projected Contributions of Computing Services to Growth in Net Output*[a]

	1993	2003			
Item	actual	Pessimistic	Midrange	Optimistic	Takeoff
Contributions from[b]					
Computing services[c]	.18	.11	.17	.23	.38
Hardware	.08	.04	.07	.10	.19
Software	.03	.03	.04	.06	.11
Computer-services labor	.06	.04	.06	.08	.08
Income shares[d]					
Computing services[c]	1.4	1.1	1.5	1.7	2.4
Hardware	.3	.2	.3	.4	.8
Software	.2	.2	.2	.3	.6
Computer-services labor	.8	.6	.9	1.0	1.0

Source: Methodology from Oliner and Sichel (1994). Figures differ from theirs for several reasons. For hardware and labor, differences reflect the correction of a minor programming error. Figures for software differ because the growth rates for nominal software cover a broader segment of the software market than the figures in Oliner and Sichel. Finally, the take-off scenario presented here uses a different rate of return assumption than in Oliner and Sichel.

a. Computing services include computer hardware (CPE), software, and computer-services labor.
b. Percentage point a year.
c. Components may not sum to total because of rounding.
d. Percent.

Figure 4-3. *Growth Contributions of Computing Services to Net Output*

Percentage points

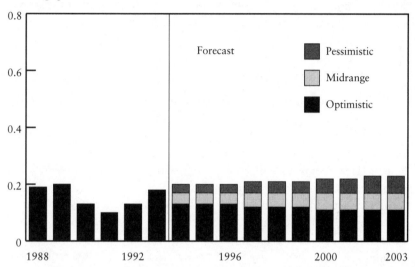

Source: Methodology from Oliner and Sichel (1994). Figures differ from theirs, reflecting a different series for software and the correction of a minor programming error.

Contributions to growth in net output are shown in table 4-4 and figure 4-3. As discussed earlier, these contributions give a better sense of contributions to welfare because they strip out the portion of the return to computers that just goes to cover costs of depreciation and obsolescence. In the optimistic scenario, the contribution to growth rises to 0.23 percentage point in 2003, somewhat above the contribution in 1993. Just as for the growth contributions calculated earlier in the chapter, once depreciation and obsolescence are netted out, the contributions of computing services to growth in the future remain modest in these three scenarios.

The key message is that even with very rapid growth of hardware, software, and labor inputs, the contribution of computing services to growth is unlikely to rise substantially in coming years, as long as computer hardware and software earn the same net return as other capital. This message undercuts the argument that computers may not have been important in the 1970s and 1980s but that with continued rapid growth they will be important in the coming decade. Even with continued rapid growth, the income shares of computing services—shown in the lower panels of table 4-3 for gross output and table 4-4 for net output—remain modest, as long as hardware and software earn a competitive return. Just as the growth-accounting analysis for the recent past placed limits on the size of computing services' contribution to growth, so too does this exercise place limits on plausible contributions for the future.

What If the Best Is Yet to Come?

The projections for these three scenarios are, of course, based on the assumption that computer hardware and software continue to earn the same competitive net rate of return as other assets. What if this assumption is wrong in a fundamental way?

Paul David, among others, has suggested that the big productivity gains from information technology are still to come.[56] He argues that radically new technologies diffuse gradually, because it takes a long time for companies to learn how to use the new resources effectively and because it may not be profitable or possible to immediately scrap the old technology. Moreover, truly revolutionary applications often require major reorganizations of production, which take a long time to discover.

David makes this argument vivid by looking back at the spread of electric motors. He notes that the main discoveries that made commercial application of electricity feasible occurred between 1856 and 1880. Early applications—such as replacement of a large steam power unit—generated only modest savings from reduced power costs. Gradually, electric power spread. By 1919 electricity accounted for 53 percent of the mechanical drive power in manufacturing. In the following decade productivity growth picked up sharply, as firms learned to reorganize production and material handling to fully exploit the new paradigm.[57]

In a casual sense, this story seems readily applicable to computers. For example, telecommuting, mobile offices, and "virtual" workplaces only now appear to be spreading rapidly. Some observers have suggested that these developments could radically reduce the need for office buildings, highways, and other physical infrastructure. Further, the explosion of computer networks, linking more and more employees within and across businesses, could generate substantial benefits through the low cost of acquiring and sharing large amounts of information. Other revolutionary applications of information technology remain to be discovered.

56. David (1989, 1990).
57. David (1989, tables 2 , 3).

However, electric power differs from desktop computers in important ways. Switching a manufacturing plant around to use electric power rather than steam power transmitted by a set of belts would have required huge expenditures to reconfigure the physical plant. Such large transition costs suggest that the transition might proceed at a modest pace and that it could take significant time until firms realized large productivity gains. In contrast, switching from mainframe computers and conventional office machines such as typewriters to desktop computers is simpler and less disruptive, suggesting a shorter lag before companies realized gains from desktop computing. To the extent that transition costs are smaller for desktop computing than for electric power, firms may already largely be realizing the gains from desktop computing, in which case there would be less reason to expect a large pickup in these gains down the road.

Whatever the answer to these questions, David's story raises the possibility that the productivity contribution of computers will rise significantly in the future. To explore this possibility, assume that the nominal net return earned by computer hardware and software rises rapidly over the next decade, doubling from a competitive rate in 1993 (estimated to be 13.2 percent in 1993) to 26.4 percent.[58] As discussed in the section on supernormal returns, there are reasons to doubt the likelihood of such a surge. Nevertheless, it is useful to examine how much of a pickup in growth contributions would be realized if such a surge were to occur. As shown by the scenario labeled "takeoff" in table 4-3 and figure 4-4 for gross output, the contribution of computing services to gross output growth rises from 0.34 percentage point in 1993 to 0.64 percentage point in 2003, a noticeable pickup.[59] As table 4-4 and figure 4-4 show for net output, computing services' contribution to growth increases from 0.18 percentage point in 1993 to 0.38 percentage point in 2003.

This take-off projection shows what must occur if the contribution of computers to output growth is to pick up substantially in coming years. To get a big pickup, the return earned by computers must surge in coming

58. Oliner and Sichel considered a scenario in which the rate of return surged up to the supernormal return implicit in Brynjolfsson and Hitt's work. As discussed earlier, however, the inclusion of software likely would reduce Brynjolfsson and Hitt's estimated rate of return to something close to the neoclassical return. Therefore, the scenario considered does not use Brynjolfsson and Hitt's estimate to calibrate possible supernormal returns for the take-off scenario.

59. Note that any supernormal returns earned by computers likely would be transitory. After some time, continued investment in hardware and software by profit-maximizing firms would be expected to drive the nominal return earned on computers back down to the level earned on other assets.

Figure 4-4. *Growth Contributions of Computing Services to Gross and Net Output (take-off scenario)*

Percentage points

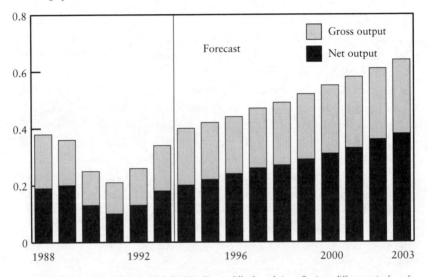

Source: Methodology from Oliner and Sichel (1994). Figures differ from theirs, reflecting a different series for software and the correction of a minor programming error.

years; continued rapid growth in the stock of computer hardware and software is not enough, as revealed by the optimistic scenario described earlier. While the scenario for takeoff is certainly a possibility, at least three reasons cast doubt on the idea that it has begun to unfold.

First, if the returns to computing hardware and software really have jumped, we should have observed a surge in the trend growth rate of the computer capital stock. As shown in figure 1-2, however, the real stock of computers appears not to have grown especially rapidly through 1995. With recent growth below the pace observed in early 1980s—and part of the pickup in the early 1990s reflecting a recovery from recession—the take-off scenario should only be regarded as a theoretical possibility for the future.

Second, if the take-off scenario is already unfolding and the return to computer investments is surging, individual companies should see the return to computers rising above that earned on other possible investments. As discussed in box 4-1, however, the evidence from the focused interviews completed for this study suggested that companies are not earning supernormal returns on information technology. To the extent that the stories in these interviews generalize to the economy as a whole, there is an additional reason to doubt that the take-off scenario is already under way.

Third, as the earlier discussion on supernormal returns made clear, a surge in the return to computer hardware and software would imply that one of two conditions hold, neither of which seems particularly plausible. Either companies are, at least ex post, behaving irrationally because they are not buying all of the computers that they should, or companies are unable to buy all of the computers that they want. That is, if the return on computers is higher than on other investments and the firm's cost of capital, then that firm would continue buying more hardware and software until computers were being used for every application that could earn a return better than that on other investments. If the firm were not doing this, it is behaving irrationally or is constrained in some way that prevents it from acting as it wishes. For the reasons described in the section on supernormal returns, neither of these conditions seems plausible. There is no evidence to show that businesses in the United States have difficulty purchasing computers, and it seems a stretch to suggest that businesses are continuing to make mistakes in their investment strategies by buying too few computers.

Moreover, when asked about barriers to progress on the information-technology front, no respondents in the focused interviews referred to difficulties of purchasing computers. Instead, respondents indicated that getting their employees up the learning curve was the biggest challenge to getting full value from information technology investments, as described in box 4-3.

Appendix: Deriving the Neoclassical Growth-Accounting Expression in Equation 4-1

The basic growth-accounting expression in equation 4-1 is formally derived here from fundamental economics.[60]

For this derivation, the usual set of neoclassical assumptions is used: (a) constant returns to scale in production; (b) the existence of competitive equilibrium, which forces the private marginal product of each factor to equal its real user cost; and (c) the absence of externalities, which eliminates any potential wedge between private and social marginal products.

---

60. The derivations in this Appendix draw heavily from Oliner and Sichel (1994), with some text taken directly (pp. 280–82, 296).

Box 4-3. *Climbing the Learning Curve*

Respondents identified many barriers to getting good payoffs from their information technology investments, including technical, organizational, and human obstacles. The one challenge that nearly every company identified and emphasized was that of getting their people up the technology learning curve; that is, the challenge of training employees to use new systems effectively and the challenge of reorganizing work to exploit the new technologies.

Among the companies only running desktop networks, Bob Womack, director of Computer Services at the law firm Hale and Dorr, put it, "The single worst problem is training and trying to get people up the [learning] curve. Getting people into a mindset where they are used to doing multiple things from their desktop is sometimes problematic. . . . These are not skills people are taught in law school." Ron Friedmann, director of Computer Applications at Wilmer, Cutler, and Pickering, echoed the same view, "The key thing is the people element . . . technology is changing faster than people can adjust and [the challenge] is, how do you bring them along."

The larger companies also identified the human challenge, as expressed in the following quotes from two different companies.[1]

Education is key. People don't know what all the tools can do. You want to get people to use these tools, but if you drop the education ball, it's not going to happen.

Getting the technology to work is very challenging, but once you've figured out those issues, the key is whether you can meet the needs of human beings in the business. If you only focus on getting technology to work, you never achieve the goal of improving productivity.

Consider the aggregate production function

$$(4A-1) \qquad\qquad Y = F(\mathbf{X},t)$$

where Y is real output, $\mathbf{X} = (X_1, X_2, \dots, X_n)$ is a vector of capital and labor inputs, and t represents shifts in the production technology over time.

One person from another large company listed several barriers to effective use of technology but put training first. When asked about where extra resources could best be deployed, this respondent also focused on training:

I think we need to throw a lot of that [extra money] at training. . . . We've given them more than they can even absorb. I think that's a big part of the technology gap right now. If we can make up that training gap, we can make another huge leap.

This last comment highlights another aspect of the learning curve barrier mentioned by many respondents. Namely, that a key factor limiting the gains from information technology is the speed with which employees can move up the learning curve. As put by one respondent at one of the smaller companies, "[We're] going as fast as we can absorb [technology], and as fast as is sensible, given the need to train people." Ron Friedmann from Wilmer, Cutler, and Pickering made the same point, "Software is evolving faster than people can buy the hardware and put it in place. Overall, [we're] more constrained by the human factor." Bob Womack at Hale and Dorr said, "I'm a technologist and I'd love to make extravagant claims for what technology can deliver. I think there are some things technology can do for you, but [success] is much more likely to depend on human or organizational factors than just on technology."

1. Some of the larger companies using mainframes also emphasized technical challenges. In particular, getting client-server technology to perform well within expected costs and the greater difficulties and risks of running systems that are far more complex than stand-alone mainframes.

Differentiate equation (4A-1) with respect to time, yielding

(4A-2) $\partial Y/\partial t = \Sigma_I (\partial F/\partial X_i)/(\partial X_i/\partial t) + (\partial F/\partial t).$

Now, divide both sides of the equation by Y, and multiply and divide each term in the summation sign by X_i, yielding

(4A-3) $\dot{Y} = \Sigma_i (\partial F/\partial X_i)(X_i/Y)\dot{X}_i + (\partial F/\partial t)/Y,$

Table 4A-1. *Forecast Assumptions for Future Growth Contributions of Computing Services, 1994–2003*

Percent change[a]

Item	Pessimistic scenario (average growth rate, 1988–93)	Midrange scenario (average growth rate, 1984–93)	Optimistic scenario (1993 growth rate)
Nominal net CPE stock	2.0	6.1	8.4
Nominal output private nonfarm business, gross	4.7	5.6	5.4
Nominal output private nonfarm business, net	4.8	5.6	6.4
Real CPE capital input	16.9	20.5	25.1
Real software input	13.8	16.7	20.4
Computer-services labor input	5.8	7.1	7.7

a. Average log differences multiplied by 100.

where the variables with dots represent growth rates which are equal to the time derivative of a variable divided by the variable's level; for example $(\partial X_i/\partial t)/X_i = \dot{X}_i$.

Let p denote the price of output. Then, assumptions (b) and (c) above imply that the social marginal product of each input $(\partial F/\partial X_i)$ equals its real factor price (r_i/p). With this substitution, we obtain

(4A-4) $$\dot{Y} = \Sigma_i \, (r_i/p)(X_i/Y)\dot{X}_i + (\partial F/\partial t)/Y,$$

Note that $r_i X_i/pY$ is the share of nominal income accruing to input i and set this equal to s_i. And, let $\dot{MFP} = (\partial F/\partial t)/Y$ represent the rate of growth in multifactor productivity; that is, the portion of output growth that is not accounted for by changes in specific inputs. With these substitutions, the expression becomes

(4A-5) $$\dot{Y} = \Sigma_i \, s_i \dot{X}_i + \dot{MFP}.$$

As these substitutions make clear, the nominal income share for each input equals its output elasticity, under neoclassical assumptions. With constant returns to scale, the income shares sum to one.

Next, make equation 4A-5 specific to three inputs: computer capital, other capital, and labor, denoted by subscripts C, O, and L, respectively. With this modification, the growth-accounting equation becomes

(4A-6) $$\dot{Y} = s_C \dot{K}_C + s_O \dot{K}_O + s_L \dot{L} + \dot{MFP}.$$

where $s_C \dot{K}_C$ is the growth contribution of computers, $(s_O \dot{K}_O)$ is the contribution of all capital other than computers, and $s_L \dot{L}$ is the contribution of aggregate labor input. Equation 4A-6 matches equation 4-1 in the text of the chapter, which describes each of the terms of equation 4A-6 in words.

Deriving the Contribution of Computing Services to Output Growth

Start with the growth accounting equation 4A-6 above that breaks out computer hardware:

(4A-7) $$\dot{Y} = s_C \dot{K}_C + s_O \dot{K}_O + s_L \dot{L} + \dot{MFP}$$

To break out computing services, add a term for the contribution of software, $s_{CS}\dot{K}_{CS}$, where s_{CS} is the income share of software and $\dot{K}_{CS}$ is the growth of the real stock of software. Split out computer-services labor from the total labor input, which entails replacing the term for total labor input with two terms: $s_{CL}\dot{L}_{CL}$ (where s_{CL} is the income share for computer-services labor and $\dot{L}_{CL}$ is the growth rate of computer-services labor) and a term for all other labor, $s_L\dot{L} - s_{CL}\dot{L}_{CL}$. Putting these pieces together yields:

$$
(4A\text{-}8) \qquad \dot{Y} = (s_C\dot{K}_C + s_{CS}\dot{K}_{CS} + s_{CL}\dot{L}_{CL}) + s_O\dot{K}_O
$$

$$
+ (s_L\dot{L} - s_{CL}\dot{L}_{CL}) + M\dot{F}P
$$

where the terms in the first set of parentheses capture the contribution of computing services to output growth.

CHAPTER 5

The Computer Revolution:
Examples from the Past

T HIS CHAPTER provides some historical perspective on recent developments in the computer revolution. The literature on the history of technology and the role of technological developments in economic growth is extensive, and this chapter does not turn over new ground on those issues. Rather, simple examples and evidence are used to highlight important continuities and parallels between recent developments in the computer revolution and past developments in office automation and elsewhere in the economy. Namely, the economy's information intensity has been on an uptrend for over one hundred and fifty years; office automation equipment was used extensively and underwent rapid technological change before the development of computers; and other important economic innovations experienced rapid price declines in earlier periods just as computing services have more recently.

These historical continuities are important because how we view recent developments in information technology affects our perceptions of the likely impacts of this technology. If recent developments were viewed as unprecedented, then expectations of a large impact on economic growth and productivity could naturally follow from that view. However, if recent developments are viewed as a steady continuation of past developments, then more muted expectations would logically follow.

Finally, media coverage of the computer revolution is examined. As discussed earlier, much recent media coverage suggests that recent developments in information technology are unprecedented and that a surge in productivity may well be on the horizon. In chapter 1, I quoted an article from *Forbes ASAP*, suggesting that "we may be on the cusp of that long-awaited productivity surge."[1] This coverage is compared with

---

1. Michael Rothschild, "The Coming Productivity Surge," *Forbes ASAP*, March 29, 1993, pp. 17–18.

commentary on computers in past decades, noting that extreme optimism has been standard fare in the media since the dawn of the computer revolution several decades ago.

The Information Revolution: The Long View

Information intensity was on an uptrend for more than a century and a half before the widespread adoption of desktop computing. Many researchers, beginning with Fritz Machlup and Daniel Bell, have assessed the importance of information in the economy.[2] Although any measure of the information intensity of an economy must be regarded as only a crude approximation, two are considered here: the share of the work force engaged in information activities and the share of the capital stock accounted for by information processing equipment. These two measures do not tell us about the economy's output of information but rather reveal the share of the economy's labor and equipment resources (inputs) devoted to information activities. All else equal, the more important are information-related activities in the economy, the greater the share of resources that would be expected to be devoted to these activities. As shown below, both measures suggest that recent increases in information labor and capital investment largely reflect a continuation of past trends. To provide another perspective, the following pages also compare recent rates of price decline in computing services to that of earlier nonoffice innovations that left important marks on previous periods.

Information Intensity: Labor and Capital Shares

For the information share of the labor force, the detailed classification developed by Marc Porat can be used. For this classification, Porat identified occupations that "are primarily engaged in the production, processing, or distribution of information."[3] This is a broad definition of the

---

2. See Bell (1973, pp. 126–27); and Machlup (1962, p. 400). For a careful historical analysis of information and technologies used for "control," see Beniger (1986). He argues that the information revolution began in the mid-nineteenth century with the rise of railroads and that recent developments represent a continuation of these past trends. Many other researchers have drawn parallels between past and recent developments. For example, see Yates (1983, 1989, 1991) on communication and tabulating technologies and David (1989, 1990) comparing the spread of computers to that of electric power.

3. Porat (1977, pp. 104–35). The quotation is on p. 105.

Table 5-1. Information-Sector Labor, 1800–1993

Year	Information-sector share (percent)	Total labor force (millions)	Number of information workers (millions)
1800	0.2	1.5	.003
1810	0.3	2.2	.006
1820	0.4	3.0	.012
1830	0.4	3.7	.015
1840	4.1	5.2	.213
1850	4.2	7.4	.310
1860	5.8	8.3	.481
1870	4.8	12.5	.600
1880	6.5	17.4	1.131
1890	12.4	22.8	2.827
1900	12.8	29.2	3.738
1910	14.9	39.8	5.930
1920	17.7	45.3	8.018
1930	24.5	51.1	12.264
1940	24.9	53.6	13.346
1950	30.8	57.8	17.802
1960	42.0	67.8	28.476
1970	46.4	80.1	37.166
1980	50.9	106.9	54.412
1990	55.2	124.8	68.889
1993	56.0	128.0	71.680

Source: Data from 1800–1970 from Beniger (1986, p. 24) based on Porat's (1977) classification. Data for 1980–93 based on author's calculation. To obtain these later figures, the 1970 share was incremented by the increase in the share of white-collar employment. Figures for the total labor force for 1980 and after are from the *Economic Report of the President, 1994*, p. 306.

information sector and includes most managers, professionals, and clerical and sales workers. In rough terms, this category covers white-collar workers.

Table 5-1 and figure 5-1, in accordance with this definition, show the share of information workers in the total U.S. labor force during the nearly two centuries between 1800 and 1993.[4] As the figure shows, this measure implies minimal information intensity before 1830, that is, before the economy had become sufficiently complex to require substantial information and coordination. Since then, this share has risen fairly steadily with jumps in the 1830s (railroads), the 1880s (rapid bureaucratization of big business), and the 1950s (postwar boom).[5] Information labor now accounts for more than half of the labor force. The increase

4. Beniger extended Porat's series back to 1800, while the figures for 1980 and afterward are based on the author's calculations, as described in the notes to table 5-1.
5. Beniger (1986, pp. 23–24).

Figure 5-1. *Information-Sector Labor, 1800–1990*

Percent of labor force

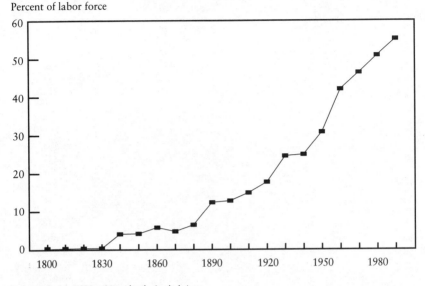

Source: Beniger (1986, p. 24); and author's calculations.

in the 1980s, although large, is similar to increases in earlier periods of rapidly growing information intensity.

For a capital-based measure of information intensity, consider the definition of information processing equipment provided by the Bureau of Economic Analysis.[6] This measure includes office, computing, and accounting machinery (OCA); communication gear; and other information processing equipment. Figure 5-2 shows the nominal share of information processing equipment out of the entire net stock of nonresidential equipment and structures.

As figure 5-2 shows, the capital stock share of information equipment also has increased substantially since 1925, from under 2 percent in 1925 to nearly 12 percent by 1993.[7] In the 1920s and 1930s, this share re-

6. U.S. Department of Commerce (1993) and updates.
7. If this share were shown in constant 1987 dollars, the increase since 1925 and after 1987 would be more dramatic because of the rapid price declines experienced by computers. Such constant-dollar shares, however, would be arbitrary and misleading, as discussed in the Appendix to chapter 3. Calculating 1987 dollar shares for office equipment amounts to valuing the stock of office equipment in other years at 1987 prices. But what does it mean to evaluate office equipment in the 1930s at 1987 prices? Most products purchased in the 1930s were not available in 1987, and most products purchased in 1987 were not

Figure 5-2. *Information Processing Equipment as a Share of the Nominal Net Capital Stock, 1925–93*

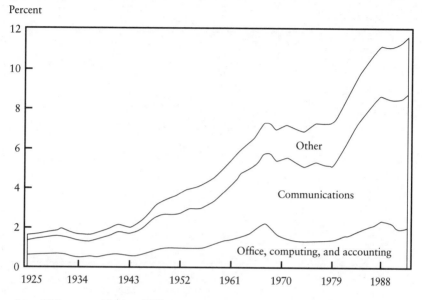

Percent

Source: U.S. Department of Commerce (1993).

mained fairly flat and then turned up sharply during the 1950s and 1960s. Surprisingly, this share went nowhere in the 1970s, before turning up sharply in the 1980s. Although the upturn in this share in the 1980s is steeper than in earlier decades, there were substantial runups in earlier periods as well. Moreover—as revealed by the category detail in the figure 5-2—the jump in the 1980s reflected a surge in communication equipment, not computers.

---

available in the 1930s. To avoid this problem, it is more appropriate to do comparisons over long spans of history, using nominal shares, which indicate the fraction of the capital stock devoted to a particular asset each year *evaluated at the prices purchasers faced in that year*. Moreover, the choice of 1987 as a base year is arbitrary. We could just as well choose 1950 as a base year. In that year, computers were much more expensive than in later years. Thus the stock of computers in 1990, calculated in the prices of 1950, would be very valuable indeed, making its share in the capital stock appear very large. Alternatively, we could value the 1990 stock of computers at prices expected to prevail in the year 2000. Because computer prices are likely to fall further, this would make the 1990 stock of computers, and its share in the capital stock, look quite small. As discussed in the Appendix to chapter 3, constant-dollar figures are completely appropriate for certain uses, but not for measuring capital stock shares.

Figure 5-3. *Information Technology Spending and Output per Capita, Selected OECD Countries, 1991*

GDP per capita, 1991 (dollars)

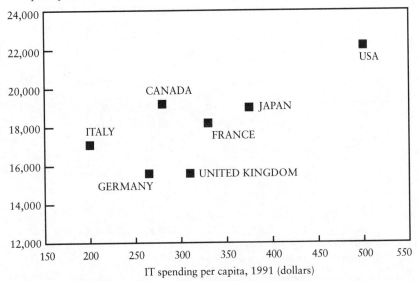

IT spending per capita, 1991 (dollars)

Source: OECD (1994, fig. 4). In the OECD data, information technology includes computer hardware, software, communication equipment linked and used specifically with computer devices, and computer support services. Figures are in current U.S. dollars, converted using purchasing power parity conversion factors.

Does Greater Information Intensity Lead to Faster Economic Growth?

The data presented so far suggest that recent developments in information technology—at least as captured by labor and capital inputs—represent a broad continuation of historical trends. These broad trends suggest that greater information intensity has not been associated with faster economic growth in the past. At the simplest level, figures 5-1 and 5-2 demonstrate this point. As these figures show, the information intensity of the economy has increased substantially since the middle of the nineteenth century, but there has not been a commensurate and steady increase in the economy's trend growth rate. Rather, the figures suggest that an economy's information intensity is related more to its overall size than to its rate of growth.

The same relationship emerges from a cross-section of international data. Figure 5-3, focusing on the seven major industrialized economies, reveals a strong relationship between the level of per capita spending on

Figure 5-4. *Information Technology Spending and Productivity Growth, Selected OECD Countries, 1991*

Productivity growth, annual average, 1984–94 (percent)

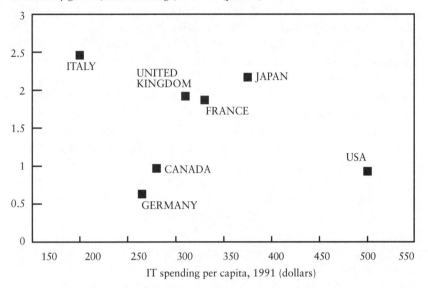

IT spending per capita, 1991 (dollars)

Source: IT spending per capita from OECD (1994, fig. 4). Productivity growth from *OECD Economic Outlook.*

information technology and the *level* of per capita output in 1991; that is, higher-income economies tend to purchase more information technology.

However, per capita spending on information technology seems not to be related to *growth rates* of productivity across the same group of countries, as shown in figure 5-4. This figure plots the level of per capita spending on information technology in 1991 against average growth rates of productivity between 1984 and 1994.[8] As the figure shows, there is little correlation between this measure of information intensity and productivity growth, implying that information intensity alone is not the source of faster growth.[9]

8. The period from 1984 to 1994 was used to avoid picking up cyclical effects and to provide some coverage on each side of the 1991 figures for per capita information technology spending.

9. This evidence is similar to evidence for the United States that examines the relationship between information technology and economic growth across industries. Using conventional measures, there is little correlation, although Popkin (1992) has suggested that misallocation of output among industries might account for this lack of correlation.

Comparing the Pace of Price Decline for Computing Services to Three Earlier Innovations

Although there are many ways to gauge technological advance, changes in quality-adjusted prices provide a useful metric that is often applied to computers; these measures show the speed at which price-performance ratios improve. In this spirit, this section compares the pace of price decline for computing services to that for rail transit in the nineteenth century and electricity and airline travel in this century. The railroad comparison is interesting because railroads are often thought of as a key element in the industrial revolution in the United States in the nineteenth century, although the role of railroads in economic growth has been keenly debated.[10] The electricity comparison is interesting because the spread of electricity has been used as a historical analogy for the development of computers.[11] Finally, the airline comparison is helpful because it is closer in time than the others to the beginning of the computer age.

Before describing these comparisons, three conceptual issues must be discussed. First, each of these services is the joint product of machinery, buildings, materials, energy, and labor. Purchasers of these services are concerned about the final price, not the price of inputs such as locomotives or aircraft. Similarly, businesses using computers are (or should be) concerned about the price of the entire package of computing services as actually used, not the price of hardware alone. Thus, the appropriate computer-related price for this comparison is that of computing services, which is just the series developed in chapter 3.

Second, to do these comparisons appropriately, price changes must be adjusted for the overall rate of inflation in each different historical period; that is, real price changes should be compared. Third, potential mismeasurement of these price changes means that these comparisons should be taken as only suggestive. In particular, prices for rail and air transit are not quality adjusted, and on a quality-adjusted basis prices probably have fallen faster than the figures shown in the table. For example, the rail passenger fare in 1890 is for a far more comfortable and speedier trip than the much higher rate earlier in that century. And even though the prices of

---

10. For example, Rostow (1960, p. 55) argues that railroads triggered the "takeoff" in growth in the nineteenth century. Fogel (1964), however, put forward a compelling argument that earlier analysts had overstated the role of railroads.

11. David (1990).

the hardware and software components of computing services were quality adjusted, there is still scope for substantial mismeasurement.

Table 5-2 shows these historical comparisons of price changes. As shown in the first row, the nominal price of computing services is estimated to have fallen 4.4 percent between 1987 and 1993, while the real (or inflation-adjusted) price fell almost 8 percent. In comparison, real electricity prices fell at an annual rate of 7 percent in the first half of this century, nearly as rapidly as the decline in the price of computing services since 1987. Real prices of rail and air transit also fell notably in earlier periods, although at a less rapid pace than computing services. Remember, however, that the reported decline in rail and air transit prices likely understates the actual decline because these prices were not quality adjusted.

Taken together, these comparisons suggest that services that underwent substantial innovation in earlier historical periods experienced rapid real price declines, just as did computing services—including hardware, software, and labor inputs—in the more recent period.

Office Automation Equipment before Computers

This section provides some historical examples to highlight that the business sector used office-automation equipment extensively long before the advent of computers.[12] A look at the capital-stock shares in figure 5-2 confirms this fact. The lower line in the figure shows the capital-stock share of office, computing, and accounting equipment dating back to 1925, confirming its extensive use in earlier periods. The office equipment share of the capital stock had attained half of its current value by 1950, *before the widespread adoption of electronic computers.* At that time, this category included typewriters, arithmetic calculating machines, card-based tabulating machinery, accounting equipment, and other automatic information equipment. Clearly, businesses were using this precomputer equipment in substantial quantities.

Figure 5-2 also indicates that increases in the office-equipment intensity of the economy tended to come in waves. Since the advent of computers, the share of office, computing, and accounting machinery has not trended steadily upward. Instead, there was a notable runup during the

12. Cortada (1993b) and Flamm (1987, 1988) provide excellent historical background on computers in their early years.

Table 5-2. *Real Price Changes for Computing Services, Electricity, Rail Transit, and Airline Transit, Various Periods*

Item	Period of coverage	Observed price change (percent, annual rate)	GDP or GNP deflator (percent, annual rate)	Real price change (percent, annual rate)
Computing services	1987–1993	–4.4	3.5	–7.9
Electricity	1899–1948	–4.5	2.5	–7.0
Rail transit	1850–1890	–2.7	0.0	–2.7
Airline transit	1935–1948	0.2	5.0	–4.8

Source: Computing services prices from table 3-4. Electricity prices from Gordon (1992). Airline transit prices from Gordon (1991). Rail transit prices from Fishlow (1966, p. 585); the figures in the table aggregate Fishlow's prices for freight and passenger rates using a Tornquist index. Real price changes equal nominal price changes less change in GNP or GDP deflator. For 1850–1890, the GNP price deflator is from Gallman (1966). For 1899–1929, the GNP price deflator is from Balke and Gordon (1989), and for 1929–1993, the GDP price deflator is from U.S. Department of Commerce (1992) and *Survey of Current Business*.

1950s and 1960s as large-scale computers first became available. Then in the 1970s, the share of the total capital stock accounted for by OCA actually dropped back. As desktop computing became widely available in the 1980s, this share picked up again. The behavior in the 1980s is not at all unusual from a historical perspective.

The broad trends just described are made more vivid by examining some technologies that were early precursors of desktop computers: typewriters, adding and calculating machines, punched-card tabulating machines, and the telegraph. These technologies performed many of the functions that today are integrated into desktop computers: input-output, processing of information, and communication.

With a complete historical record, the pace of technical advance for each of these technologies and functions could be tracked over time with price-performance ratios or quality-adjusted price indexes. Such measures could be used to assess whether and how much the pace of advance has picked up since the advent of computers. Developing such measures for the earlier period, however, would be extremely difficult and in many cases impossible because of data limitations. Rather than strive to develop such measures, three types of indirect evidence are presented to make the simpler points that office-automation equipment was used extensively before computers, that these technologies were quite innovative in their day, and that they underwent substantial technical improvements before the advent of computers.

The first type of evidence draws on product descriptions over time, which can be used to assess improvements in performance. Second, rapid growth of sales provides evidence that these products satisfied an important business need at a lower price than available alternatives. Third, and closely related to the second point, the large size and dramatic growth of the companies that manufactured this early equipment provides evidence that this equipment played an important role in the economy.

Typewriters

Although primitive by today's standards, typewriters made it possible for individual office workers to produce standardized printed output.[13] Once patented in 1868, typewriters underwent fairly rapid change, roughly reaching their modern form in the 1890s.[14] By the 1890s, ma-

---

13. Except where noted, the history of typewriters is primarily from Cortada (1993a, chap. 1).

14. Cortada (1993a, p. 16).

chines had QWERTY keyboards, upper- and lower-case type, spacebars, and typed text visible to the typist; the earliest machines did not have these features.

How big an innovation were typewriters for the input-output function? According to one estimate, typewriters were three times faster than handwriting by the 1890s.[15] In any case, there had been sufficient innovation by 1910 to have generated 6,200 patents for typewriters.[16]

Furthermore, demand for this automation of input-output was sufficient to boost sales rapidly. Between 1900 and 1921—the earliest years for which data are available—the annual production of typewriters in the United States more than tripled to nearly one-half million. By the end of the 1920s, production had doubled again to nearly one million units a year in an economy with about 12.5 million information workers.[17] By this time, typewriters were ubiquitous.

Related Duplicating Technologies

Duplicating technologies also advanced rapidly in this period. With the advent of carbon paper in 1872, individual office workers could produce multiple copies of documents.[18] Copying technology took another step forward in 1890 when A. B. Dick began selling mimeograph machines on a wide scale.[19] The speed of printing increased dramatically in this period.

By 1875 the new Hoe Web Printing Machine—with cylindrical printing plates—could print 25,000 pages in an hour, ten times more than its immediate technological predecessors. By 1893 the fastest machines could print 96,000 eight-page copies in an hour, a further thirtyfold increase in speed per page printed.[20] Between 1875 and 1893, the increase in printing speed represented an annual rate of 21 percent, fairly impressive even by the standards of modern computers.

Adding and Calculating Equipment

Commercial availability of these technologies began with adding machines in the 1880s and progressed through very complicated punched-

15. Yates and Benjamin (1991, p. 87).
16. Cortada (1993a, p. 21).
17. U.S. Department of Commerce (1975, part 2, p. 695).
18. Beniger (1986, p. 282).
19. Beniger (1986, p. 395).
20. The basic facts about printing technology are from Beniger (1986, p. 286).

card equipment used in the early 1950s. The first widely used adding machine was the Felt Comptometer, introduced in the late 1880s, which could add and subtract. Before this development, many office workers spent long hours calculating figures by hand. By 1890 multiplying machines were available, and four-function calculators appeared in 1893.[21] During the first part of the twentieth century, these machines gained printing capabilities, became smaller, and were electrified.

Between 1896 and 1900, the average price for an adding or calculating machine produced by the American Arithmometer Company (which later became Burroughs) was about $220, roughly equivalent to $4,000 at today's price level. Nevertheless, these machines sold like hotcakes, undoubtedly reflecting strong demand for automated calculation and suggesting that those machines represented an important technological advance. American Arithmometer's unit sales of adding and calculating machines increased at an annual rate of 32 percent between 1896 and 1900.[22]

On top of adding machines, many other office functions also were automated using similar technologies, including the generation of bills, posting of balances to account records, check writing, time posting, and recording of sales by cash registers.[23] However, the technology that changed the most over the first half of this century was punched-card equipment.[24]

Punched-Card Tabulating Equipment

The earliest punched-card machine was developed in the 1880s by Herman Hollerith.[25] For the first time, large amounts of data could be automatically stored, retrieved, sorted, and tabulated. Because this equipment was so important—and the most obvious precursor to electronic

21. Except where noted, Cortada (1993a, chap. 2) is the source of information about adding and calculating machines. See especially the chronology on p. 30.
22. The sales figures and average price for the American Arithmometer Company are from Cortada (1993a, p. 34). The adjustment to current dollars is based on the Wholesale Price Index from 1898 to 1929 and the GDP implicit price deflator from 1929 to 1993. These price figures are from U.S. Department of Commerce (1975, part 1, pp. 197, 199) and *Economic Report of the President, 1994*, p. 272. Over this period, the overall price level increased more than eighteen times.
23. Cortada (1993a, p. 159).
24. The material on punched-card equipment is from Cortada (1993a, chap. 3); and Beniger, (1986, chap. 9).
25. Cortada (1993a, p. 47).

computers—many specific applications are described by historians. These examples provide a ready vehicle for illustrating the capabilities, pervasiveness, and innovativeness of punched-card equipment.

The first large application of punched-card tabulating equipment was the 1890 U.S. Census. The 1880 Census—which was compiled by hand—was not completed until 1889. The next Census was to include twenty more items, raising the possibility that it could not be completed in ten years. The Census Bureau set up a test to compare Hollerith's equipment to manual methods, and Hollerith's equipment was almost twice as fast as the best manual method. Thus the 1890 Census was compiled automatically on ninety-six of Hollerith's tabulating machines. These machines allowed many additional subcategories to be tabulated. Even with the extra items and extra categories of tabulation, the compilation took seven years rather than nine, and contemporary observers estimated that his equipment saved $5 million, equivalent to about $90 million today.[26]

The 1900 Census also was compiled on Hollerith's machines, and by this time the price-performance ratio of the equipment had already improved substantially.[27] In 1890 the Census Bureau paid an annual rental fee of $1,000 for each machine. By 1900 the Census Bureau also used some newer machines at an annual rental rate of $1,500. Although one-and-a-half times more expensive, these machines were six times faster than the 1890 version, implying a fourfold reduction in the price-performance ratio over a ten-year period. This improvement represents an annual decline of about 14 percent in the price-performance ratio of these machines, remarkably similar to the 13 percent annual pace of decline in computer prices during the 1980s.[28]

The private sector quickly saw the advantages of this equipment as well. In the early 1900s, Marshall Field, the Chicago retailer, was recording information on 10,000 punch cards each day. In 1907 the Southern Railway Company used more than 200,000 cards a month; later, they were recording data on 550,000 cards a month. During 1910 and the first half of 1911, rentals and sales of Hollerith's firm—the Tabulat-

26. Cortada (1993a, p. 48); and Beniger (1986, pp. 413–14). The adjustment to current dollars assumes an eighteenfold increase in prices since the mid-1890s, the same figure used earlier.

27. Data about the tabulation of the 1900 Census is from Cortada (1993a, p. 53).

28. The annual pace of decline for the 1890s is calculated as a log difference. The figure for computer prices in the 1980s is from table 1-1, also calculated as a log difference.

ing Machine Company—increased about 20 percent every six months.[29] More generally, the range of applications for which this equipment was used in the business sector sounds surprisingly similar to that of modern information technology: inventory and warehouse management, payroll analysis, production accounting, sales projections, market forecasting, and maintaining purchase records.[30]

One additional government application is worth noting. In the 1930s, the new Social Security Administration needed to keep track of 26 million Americans. To do this, they installed 415 punched-card machines. The first social security check—issued in 1937—was printed on a punch card. Automatic information processing was already commonplace in America.[31]

The Telegraph

Communications gear represents another strand of technology that has merged into modern information processing equipment.[32] Although the speed and available bandwidth of communication has increased greatly in recent years, important early improvements occurred in the nineteenth century with the development of the telegraph and telephone, coinciding with the need for greater control and coordination of an increasingly complex economy.

In an interesting example, JoAnne Yates and Robert I. Benjamin put some numbers on increases in the speed of communication.[33] They estimated that sending a one-page message from New York to Chicago took more than ten days in the 1840s before railroads were widespread. After the telegraph was available in the 1850s, they estimate that the same message could be sent in about five minutes, better than a three-thousandfold increase in speed. They also estimated that the cost of sending the message in the 1840s was twenty-five cents for a postage stamp, while the cost of the telegraphic message in the 1850s was about $7.50. After taking cost into account, the price-speed ratio improved by a factor of 100 over roughly ten years, which is a remarkable figure even by today's standards of technical advance.

29. Cortada (1993a, pp. 53,55).
30. Cortada (1993a, pp. 50, 131).
31. These facts on social security are from Beniger (1986, pp. 408, 409).
32. This chronology is taken from Beniger (1986, pp. 234, 325–26).
33. Yates and Benjamin (1991, p. 72).

The Companies That Produced Office-Automation Equipment

This discussion of information processing functions suggests that office-automation equipment was used extensively and underwent substantial innovation long before computers came on the scene. That office-automation equipment played an important role in the economy can be seen another way as well. Often, companies that develop innovative and important products grow rapidly and—at least for a while—are very successful. For example, companies like Microsoft, Intel, Apple, Motorola, IBM, and DEC have been seen at various times as symbols of the importance and innovativeness of information technology. Similar patterns can be seen in the office automation business earlier in the century, bolstering the idea that the earlier equipment was quite innovative in its day, too.

Before World War II, the companies that produced office-automation equipment were already big players in the economy and were growing rapidly. In 1917 the Remington typewriter company and Burroughs Adding Machine Company were among the 200 largest companies in the United States. By 1930 IBM (which by that time had absorbed Hollerith's tabulating machine company), National Cash Register, and the Underwood typewriter company were also among the nation's largest companies.[34] And, by the early 1930s, the Justice Department had already filed an antitrust suit against IBM for unfair practices in the punched-card equipment market.[35] Clearly, office automation was already big business in these earlier periods.

Past Commentary on the Computer Revolution

Since the 1950s the business press has taken a keen interest in computers. Strong parallels can be seen between that commentary and much discussion in today's media. The rest of this section compares a few examples of this commentary from the late 1950s and late 1960s to commentary in the early 1990s. The 1950s and 1960s were chosen because they predate the productivity slowdown of the 1970s and more recent concerns about the productivity performance of computers. Even in that very different era, stories bore striking similarities to those written more re-

34. Cortada (1993a, p. 153).
35. Cortada (1993a, p. 116).

cently. The older stories typically recount recent difficulties companies had encountered in getting good payoffs from computers; nonetheless the stories ended with an optimistic assessment of future gains.

The Late 1950s

On June 21, 1958, *Business Week* published a special report on computers.[36] The story began by noting that earlier applications of computers had encountered some difficulties. "Computers are no strangers in business today—but the new industrial revolution they herald has hardly begun. Their real potential has been snagged in false starts and mistakes in use—but they're on their way." To bolster the claims about recent difficulties, *Business Week* continued, "Out of a welter of exaggerated claims in the earlier years, there has been growing a more recent chorus of complaint. Costs were higher than had been estimated. Results fell far short of expectations. In a recent survey, a solid 40 percent of computer users talked of 'disappointment.'" Why? *Business Week* pointed to business organization, noting that overcoming these problems would require "the radical reorganization of the corporation as it now exists."[37]

Despite these difficulties, *Business Week* hit a couple of optimistic notes in the conclusion. The story draws out the implications of a younger, more computer-literate crowd moving up: "Today's old-timers will be gone—and today's computer kids will sit in their place. Some of the dreams will come true." The story ended with a fanciful example of how computers might end the business cycle: "extensions of today's 'faster reports' might even some day beat the business cycle. . . . Neither the hardware, the manpower, nor the money for such tremendous applications are available today. But they will be."[38]

Business Week was not alone. On February 9, 1959, *Barron's* published a progress report on computers.[39] This story also noted some recent dissatisfaction with computers: "The increasing squeeze on profits [from the recent recession] made many a management unusually touchy . . . [and] many began to complain early last year that the big brains only caused bigger headaches." But *Barron's* reported that there had recently

36. "Business Week Reports to Readers on: Computers," *Business Week*, Special Report, June 21, 1958, pp. 68–92.
37. "Business Week Reports," pp. 69, 70, 72.
38. "Business Week Reports," pp. 90, 92.
39. J. Richard Elliot Jr., "Progress in Computers: A Stronger Industry Is Turning Out Smarter Electronic Brains," *Barron's*, February 9, 1959, pp. 3, 13–20.

been substantial improvements in hardware: "If the industry itself has undergone some fairly drastic changes in recent months, so too have its products. Here two of the significant trends are toward miniaturization and ultra-high speed." For example, "The conspicuous advantage of Philco's *Transac S-2000* over other large-scale machines was the reduction of its central unit to about one-tenth their size. . . . Power requirements, too, were cut drastically." With these new technologies, *Barron's* reported that dramatic payoffs were possible, citing that "National's system, keyed to its *304*, will prepare customers' statements at the rate of 50 a minute—25 times faster than present methods."

Given these developments, *Barron's* looked to the future with confidence: "The computer industry, then, still is reaching out for new worlds to conquer. . . . All in all, the stage is set for another decade of spectacular progress for the electronic brains."[40]

The Late 1960s

In August 1968, *Fortune* published a review of the computer industry that echoed many of the themes in the *Business Week* and *Barron's* stories of a decade earlier.[41] Noting the difficulties of getting good payoffs from computers, the story reported, "Every now and then some observer of the computer industry points to a cloud—small yet vaguely threatening—that sometimes appears to hang over its future. . . . Until fairly recently, most business computer applications were devoted to relatively routine, well-structured jobs such as billing and invoicing, in which they paid off measurably and handsomely. As computers grew more complex and expensive . . . the payoff became less easy to achieve and more difficult to measure."[42]

To back this up, *Fortune* cited a study done by a management consultant who found that "in thirty-six large U.S. and European companies . . . mounting computer expenses are no longer matched by rising economic returns. 'From a profit standpoint . . . computer efforts in all but a few exceptional companies are in real, if often unacknowledged, trouble.'" But this consultant ended his study on a positive note. "As yet, the real profit potential of the computer has barely begun to be tapped."[43]

40. Elliot, "Progress in Computers," pp. 13, 18, 20.
41. Gilbert Burck, "The Computer Industry's Great Expectations," *Fortune*, August 1968, pp. 92–146.
42. Burck, "The Computer Industry's Great Expectations," p. 146.
43. Burck, "The Computer Industry's Great Expectations," p. 146.

Echoing this consultant, *Fortune* concluded its story optimistically too: "Precisely because the potentialities of the computer have been only partly realized so far, the industry is sure that the business market for its computer systems will grow faster than business itself . . . [but this growth] will depend to a large degree on how well the industry can show customers . . . [how] to make full use of the computer's marvelous capacity to provide solutions."[44]

The 1990s

In the 1990s business magazines have been writing stories remarkably similar to those of earlier decades. For example, reconsider the two quotes at the beginning of the first chapter. From *Business Week* in 1994, "the productivity surge of the last two years . . . may reflect the efforts of U.S. companies to finally take full advantage of the huge sums they've spent purchasing information technology."[45] And from *Forbes ASAP* in 1993, "We may be on the cusp of that long-awaited productivity surge. The explosive growth of PCs, workstations, LANs, WANs, fiber optics, wireless communications and object-oriented software may be completing the new office paradigm."[46] These quotes fit the pattern: there have been problems in the past, but with the spectacular new technologies now in place, the real gains are under way or just around the corner. Perhaps the optimists are right this time. But perhaps this type of media coverage should be taken with a large grain of salt. Business magazines have been writing stories like this for decades, long before the development of desktop computing.

Conclusion

With more and more computing power available at lower and lower prices, many commentators have pointed to computers as a key factor powering an anticipated resurgence in productivity growth and living standards. Assessing the likelihood of this outcome requires an understanding of the links between information technology and aggregate eco-

---

44. Burck, "The Computer Industry's Great Expectations," p. 146.
45. Michael J. Mandel, "The Digital Juggernaut," *Business Week*, May 1, 1994, p. 23.
46. Michael Rothschild, "The Coming Productivity Surge," *Forbes ASAP*, March 29, 1993, pp. 17, 18.

nomic growth. Although this book does not present new research on these issues, it offers an economic framework through which these issues can be more deeply understood. The basic economic linkages between computers and aggregate economic growth are described and a cautionary guide provided on the plausible size of computers' contributions to economic growth. The analysis also highlights what would have to happen in coming years for these contributions to increase significantly.

In sum, computer hardware's contribution to aggregate economic growth is limited by its small share of the capital stock. Between 1987 and 1993, the real output of the nonfarm business sector increased at an average annual rate of 2.0 percent. Owing to computer hardware's small share of the capital stock, however, hardware is estimated to have contributed only 0.15 percentage point to this growth, on the assumption that computers earn a competitive return. Even if computers earned a higher return than other investments that companies might make, computer hardware's contribution would still be limited by its small share of the nation's productive resources. Of course, any task completed with a computer requires software and labor inputs as well as hardware. Considering the full package of computing services—including hardware, software, and labor inputs—roughly doubles the contribution of hardware just mentioned to 0.3 percentage point a year.

Although even a contribution of 0.3 percentage point a year would cumulate to many billions of dollars over time, such a contribution remains modest when compared with the slowdown in the pace of productivity growth in the 1970s. In addition, about half of the contribution of computing services to aggregate economic growth goes to cover the costs of depreciation and obsolescence of computer hardware and software, reducing the amount that can actually boost the nation's living standards.

The analysis in this book indicates that continued rapid growth in the stock of computer hardware and software is not enough, by itself, to significantly boost the contribution of computing services to output growth. Unless the growth rate of business purchases picks up in an extremely dramatic fashion, the only way for computing services to contribute significantly more to output growth in the future than in the past is for the rate of return earned by hardware and software to surge in coming years. Although it is possible that this rate of return will surge in coming years, there are reasons to doubt that such a pickup is yet under way.

A look at measurement issues shows that software is only partially included in the nation's accounting of GDP. According to rough estimates presented here, counting business purchases of software in the same way investments in hardware are counted would have boosted the annual growth rate of real business investment by as much as three-fourths of a percentage point from 1991 to 1993. For overall GDP, however, the impact is more muted. In approximate terms, covering software more completely is estimated to have boosted real GDP growth by about 0.1 percentage point a year from 1991 to 1993.

This study also examines the argument that inadequacies in the nation's tools of economic measurement mask a large contribution of computers to aggregate economic growth. Although these issues are extremely complicated and the hard evidence on either side of the debate is limited, this book argues that mismeasurement of output growth is an unlikely explanation of the apparent modest contribution of computing services to output growth or of the productivity slowdown of the 1970s.

Finally, this book highlights the important continuities between current and past developments in information technology. Businesses applied information technology extensively long before desktop computers arrived, and these earlier technologies underwent rapid innovation just as computers have more recently. These continuities are important because the way in which recent developments are viewed can heavily color the perceptions of likely impacts. In particular, if recent developments are viewed as unprecedented, then expectations of a large impact on economic growth and productivity could follow. However, if recent developments are viewed as a steady continuation of past developments, then more muted expectations might follow. Finally, one other continuity is briefly examined. Namely, that coverage of the computer revolution in the business press has been upbeat and optimistic for as long as computers have been an important business tool.

It is important for policymakers, business managers, and the general public to have reasonable expectations for the aggregate economic boost coming from information technology, especially as the Information Superhighway makes the scene. As the analysis has shown, many factors place limits on past and future contributions of computers to aggregate economic growth. Thus, even though information technologies seem to be effectively deployed in many applications and companies, some caution is in order before the nation can hope to count on a large boost to productivity growth.

Appendix: The Focused Interviews

To gain background on information technology at the company level, I conducted seven on-site interviews with a range of companies that rely on information technology. These interviews provided the material that appears in boxes throughout the book. Table A-1 summarizes key features of the companies and their information systems. As the table shows, I talked to two law firms, one engineering consulting firm, three financial services companies, and one retailer. Differences in system architecture divide these firms into two broad groups, also corresponding to the size of the companies. The law firms and the engineering firm—which are the smaller companies in terms of employment—have desktop networks. The financial services and retailing firms—which have heavy transactions loads—own or lease time on a mainframe system to which desktop equipment has been added.

The Interviews

Before the interviews, I prepared a set of questions that provided the basis for unstructured interviews. For these questions, I drew heavily from the survey work described by the National Research Council, using many very similar questions.[1] The questions used are shown below. Depending on who I was talking to and on the flow of the interview, I did not ask every respondent every question. Following the list of questions, everyone interviewed is listed. As the list indicates, I interviewed at least one person from the management side and one person from the technology side at most companies.

---

1. National Research Council (1994).

Table A-1. *Summary of Companies and Their Computer Systems*

Company	Location	Industry	Employees	Mainframe	Desktop network
Wilmer, Cutler, and Pickering	Washington, D.C.	Law	590	No	Yes
Hale and Dorr	Boston, Mass.	Law	700	No	Yes
Ross and Baruzzini	St. Louis, Mo.	Engineering	65	No	Yes
Vanguard	Valley Forge, Pa.	Financial	4,000	Yes	Yes
Mark Twain Bank	St. Louis, Mo.	Financial	1,025[a]	Yes[b]	Some
St. Paul Insurance	St. Paul, Minn.	Financial	13,000	Yes	Yes
Target Stores	Minneapolis, Minn.	Retail	30,000	Yes	Yes

Source: Author's interviews with companies. Mark Twain's employment number is from their 1993 annual report.
a. Full-time equivalent employees.
b. Mainframe time leased from a service bureau.

Questions on Overall Use of Information Technology

1. What is your company's information technology strategy? How does this strategy relate to your business strategy?
2. Describe the role of your information system within the company. What are the main functions performed by your information system?
3. What are the main technologies (hardware, software, communications links, associated processes) used for each of these functions?
4. Have there been major changes in hardware or software architecture in the past five years? Past ten years?
5. Is your use of information technology more or less intensive than your competitors in the past year? Past five years? Past ten years? Why? What are the advantages and disadvantages of your position compared to your competitors?

Questions on the Effect of Information Technology on Productivity, Performance, and Profits

1. What is the decision process for purchasing information technology? Is it different from other investments? Are the payback criteria different? How do you evaluate information technology investments once they are in place?
2. What do you estimate was the overall payoff to major investments in information technology in the last year or two, including quantifiable and intangible or non-quantifiable payoffs?
   _____ Large positive return
   _____ Modest positive return
   _____ Equal to cost of capital
   _____ Negative return
   _____ Indeterminate
3. How does this overall return compare to that generated by other investments?
4. Is the current payoff from information technology higher than five years ago? Ten years ago? If so, is the change most related to improvements in hardware, software, connectivity, training, or the company's ability to use these technologies effectively? Were changes evolutionary or sudden? If lower, what accounts for that?
5. Do you expect further improvements in the performance and payoff of information technology? Why or why not? What are the barriers to further improvement? Hardware? Software? Personnel? Other?

6. Overall, is information technology achieving the goals set by the company? Why or why not?
7. How important is information technology as a contributor to business performance and profitability compared to all other factors? What factors other than information technology were important?
8. If additional resources were available to be deployed anywhere in the company, would they go to information technology? Why? If so, where could they most effectively be deployed? Hardware, software, communications links, training, maintenance, or other aspects of information management? Why?

Questions on How Information Technology Has Changed the Business

1. What fraction of employees in each group use information technology in your company?
   _____ Management
   _____ Professional staff
   _____ Support staff
2. How have these fractions changed in the last year? Last five years? Last ten years?
3. Has information technology led to shifts in staffing away from certain functions or jobs toward others in the last year? Last five years? Last ten years?
4. Has information technology changed the skills required for certain jobs in the last year? last five years? Last ten years? Has it changed the kinds of people working here?
5. Has information technology changed the compensation or reward system for certain jobs in the last year? Last five years? Last ten years?
6. How has information technology changed the way managers, professional staff, and support staff do their jobs?
7. How has information technology changed the business?
   _____ Saving physical space
   _____ Outsourcing
   _____ Staffing
   _____ Strategic orientation
   _____ Process redesign
   _____ Customer interactions
   _____ Supplier interactions

Questions on Specific Information Technology Investments

1. What major information technology projects have been undertaken or put in place recently? (whether successful or not) When were they put in place? How large were they (dollar expenditure)?
2. What technologies (hardware, software, communications links, associated processes) were used?
3. Were these technologies purchased off the shelf? Custom developed by outside vendors? Custom developed in-house?
4. What was the primary purpose of each project?

   Cutting Costs
   ____ To save money by boosting the efficiency or reducing the cost of specific operations

   Improving Products
   ____ To expand product variety
   ____ To improve product quality
   ____ To improve timeliness of delivery
   ____ To improve products in other ways _____

   Improving Performance of Critical Business Functions
   ____ To improve interactions with customers
   ____ To improve interactions with suppliers, including EDI
   ____ To capture data on customers
   ____ To improve control and communications within the company (infrastructure)
   ____ Reengineering broader business functions to boost efficiency
   ____ To meet government-mandated requirements
   ____ Other _____

   Improving Strategic Position
   ____ To respond to competitive pressure
   ____ To reorient the strategic or competitive position of the company
   ____ Other _____
5. Have the purposes of information technology investments changed over the last five years? the last ten years? How?
6. What were the payoffs to those major information technology projects, including both quantifiable and non-quantifiable payoffs?
   ____ Large positive return
   ____ Modest positive return

_____ Equal to cost of capital
_____ Negative return
_____ Indeterminate

7. Was this payoff higher, lower, or about the same as other investments? Did the payoffs meet expectations?

8. What were the benefits that contributed to this payoff? (Use list from question 4 above) Were these mostly quantifiable or non-quantifiable?

9. Did factors related directly to the project hold down the payoffs of these projects? Did these factors relate more to hardware, software, personnel, the interface of this project with the rest of the business, or other factors? Explain.

10. Are these negative factors similar to or different from five years ago? Ten years ago?

11. For organizational issues, which aspects of the planning, design, or implementation of the project limited or facilitated success?
_____ Project size
_____ Project design
_____ Project implementation
_____ Competency of IS department
_____ Level of user involvement in design and implementation
_____ Level of user training or acceptance
_____ Management understanding of project
_____ Management support of project
_____ Process re-design

List of Interviewees by Company

Wilmer, Cutler, and Pickering, Washington, DC. Lisa B. Antel, applications consultant; Joyce D. Cutlip, director of information services; Ron Friedmann, director of computer applications; Michael Klein, managing partner; William Lake, managing partner; Jean O'Grady, librarian; and Michael Pergola, director, Advanced Applications Group.

Hale and Dorr, Boston, Massachusetts. John Hamilton, managing partner; and Bob Womack, director of computer services.

Ross and Baruzzini, St. Louis, Missouri. Maurice V. Garoutte, senior systems analyst; Carl V. Hauck, president, Missouri Division; Donald K. Ross, chairman and CEO; and Craig Toder, president.

Vanguard, Valley Forge, Pennsylvania. Tom Grace, vice president, Individual Division; Brian Henderson, vice president, Individual Division; Ralph Packard, senior vice president and chief financial officer, Tom

Satterthwaite, principal, Select Plans; and Karen West, vice president, Fund Financial Services.

The St. Paul Companies, Personal and Business Insurance Subsidiary, St. Paul, Minnesota. Deb Briskey, vice president, Marketing and Underwriting; Jim Crist, product development and compliance officer; Tom Gag, vice president, Claim Operation; Gary Hanson, president, Personal and Business Insurance; Wayne Hoeschen, senior vice president, Information Services; Mark Klein, automation services officer; Barb Lynch, Automation and Development Services; and John Wilcoxon, agency interface manager.

Mark Twain Bancshares, St. Louis, Missouri. Kevin J. Cody, vice president, chief financial officer; John Dubinsky, president; and Keith Miller, chief financial officer.

Target Stores, Minneapolis, Minnesota. Brigid A. Bonner, director, Planning, Information Management and Emerging Technologies; Paul Singer, vice president of Systems and Technology; and Bekka Trippet, project manager, Electronic Commerce.

References

Baily, Martin Neil, and Robert J. Gordon. 1988. "The Productivity Slowdown, Measurement Issues, and the Explosion of Computer Power." *Brookings Papers on Economic Activity* 2:347–420.

Baily, Martin, and James Brian Quinn. 1994. "Information Technology: The Key to Service Productivity." *Brookings Review* 12 (Summer): 37–41.

Balke, Nathan S., and Robert J. Gordon. 1989. "The Estimation of Prewar Gross National Product: Methodology and New Evidence." *Journal of Political Economy* 97 (February): 38–92.

Bell, Daniel. 1976. *The Coming of Post-Industrial Society: A Venture in Social Forecasting.* Basic Books.

Beniger, James R. 1986. *The Control Revolution: Technological and Economic Origins of the Information Society.* Harvard University Press.

Berndt, Ernst R., Zvi Griliches, and Neal Rappaport. 1995. "Econometric Estimates of Price Indexes for Personal Computers in the 1990s." *Journal of Econometrics* 68 (July): 243–68.

Boskin, Michael and others. 1996. Advisory Commission to Study the Consumer Price Index. *Toward a More Accurate Measure of the Cost of Living.* Final Report to the Senate Finance Committee. Washington. December 4.

Bound, John and George Johnson. 1992. "Changes in the Structure of Wages in the 1980s: An Evaluation of Alternative Explanations." *American Economic Review* 82 (June): 371–92.

Bresnahan, Timothy F., Paul Milgrom, and Jonathan Paul. 1992. "The Real Output of the Stock Exchange." In *Output Measurement in the Service Sectors,* edited by Zvi Griliches, 195–216. University of Chicago Press.

Brynjolfsson, Erik. 1993. "The Productivity Paradox of Information Technology." *Communications of the Association for Computing Machinery* (December): 66–77.

———, and Lorin Hitt. 1996. "Paradox Lost? Firm-Level Evidence of High Returns to Information Systems Spending." *Management Science* (April).

Brynjolfsson, Erik, and Chris F. Kemerer. 1996. "Network Externalities in Microcomputer Software: An Econometric Analysis of the Spreadsheet Market." *Management Science* 42 (December): 1627–47.

Cortada, James W. 1993a. *Before the Computer: IBM, NCR, Burroughs, and Remington Rand and the Industry They Created, 1865–1956*. Princeton University Press.

————. 1993b. *The Computer in the United States: From Laboratory to Market, 1930 to 1960*. M.E. Sharpe.

David, Paul A. 1989. "Computer and Dynamo: The Modern Productivity Paradox in a Not-Too Distant Mirror." Warwick Economic Research Papers 339. University of Warwick, Coventry.

————. 1990. "The Dynamo and the Computer: An Historical Perspective on the Modern Productivity Paradox." *American Economic Review* 80 (May): 355–61.

DeLong, J. Bradford, and Lawrence H. Summers. 1991. "Equipment Investment and Economic Growth." *Quarterly Journal of Economics* 106 (May): 445–502.

————. 1992. "Equipment Investment and Economic Growth: How Strong Is the Nexus?" *Brookings Papers on Economic Activity* 2:157–212.

Denison, Edward F. 1985. *Trends in American Economic Growth, 1929–1982*. Brookings.

————. 1989. *Estimates of Productivity Change by Industry: An Evaluation and an Alternative*. Brookings.

Digital Information Group. 1993. *Software Industry Factbook*. Stamford, Conn.

DiNardo, John, and Jorn-Steffen Pischke. 1996. "The Returns to Computer Use Revisited: Have Pencils Changed the Wage Structure Too?" Working Paper 650. Cambridge, Mass.: National Bureau of Economic Research (June).

Dulberger, Ellen R. 1989. "The Application of a Hedonic Model to a Quality-Adjusted Price Index for Computer Processors." In *Technology and Capital Formation*, edited by Dale Jorgenson and Ralph Landau, 37–75. MIT Press.

Fishlow, Albert. 1966. "Productivity and Technological Change in the Railroad Sector, 1840–1910." In *Output, Employment, and Productivity in the United States after 1800*, 583–646. NBER Studies in Income and Wealth, vol. 30. Columbia University Press.

Flamm, Kenneth. 1987. *Targeting the Computer: Government Support and International Competition*. Brookings.

————. 1988. *Creating the Computer: Government, Industry, and High Technology*. Brookings.

Fogel, Robert, W. 1964. *Railroads and American Economic Growth: Essays in Econometric History*. Johns Hopkins University Press.

Gallman, Robert E. 1966. "Gross National Product in the United States, 1834–1909." In *Output, Employment, and Productivity in the United States after*

1800, 3–75. NBER Studies in Income and Wealth, vol 30. Columbia University Press.

Gandal, Neil, 1994. "Hedonic Price Indexes for Spreadsheets and an Empirical Test for Network Externalities." *Rand Journal of Economics* 25 (Spring): 160–70.

Gordon, Robert J. 1990. *The Measurement of Durable Goods Prices*. University of Chicago Press and the National Bureau of Economic Research.

———. 1992a. "Forward into the Past: Productivity Retrogression in the Electric Generating Industry." Working Paper 3988. Cambridge, Mass.: National Bureau of Economic Research (February).

———. 1992b. "Productivity in the Transportation Sector." In *Output Measurement in the Service Sectors*, edited by Zvi Griliches, 371–422. NBER Studies in Income and Wealth. University of Chicago Press.

———. 1993. "The Jobless Recovery: Does It Signal A New Era of Productivity-Led Growth?" *Brookings Papers on Economic Activity* 1:271–306.

———. 1996. "Problems in the Measurement and Performance of Service-Sector Productivity in the United States." Working Paper 5519. Cambridge, Mass.: National Bureau of Economic Research (March).

Griliches, Zvi. 1994. "Productivity, R&D and the Data Constraint." *American Economic Review* 84 (March): 1–23.

Gurbaxani, Vijay C. 1990. *Managing Information Systems Costs: An Economic Analysis of Hardware/Software Trade-Offs*. Washington: International Center for Information Technologies.

Hulten, Charles R. 1992. "Accounting for the Wealth of Nations: The Net Versus Gross Output Controversy and Its Ramifications." *Scandinavian Journal of Economics* 94 Supplement: 9–24.

Krohe, James Jr. 1993. "The Productivity Pit: Evaluating the Effectiveness of Computers." *Across the Board* 30 (October): 16–21.

Krueger, Alan B. 1993. "How Computers Have Changed the Wage Structure: Evidence from MicroData, 1984–1989." *Quarterly Journal of Economics* 108 (February): 33–60.

Lau, Lawrence J., and Ichiro Tokutsu. 1992. "The Impact of Computer Technology on the Aggregate Productivity of the United States: An Indirect Approach." Mimeo. Stanford University (August).

Lebow, David E., John M. Roberts, and David J. Stockton. 1992. "Economic Performance under Price Stability." Economic Activity Section Working Paper 125. Board of Governors of the Federal Reserve System (April).

Lichtenberg, Frank R. 1995. "The Output Contributions of Computer Equipment and Personnel: A Firm-Level Analysis." *Economics of Innovation and New Technology* 3 (3-4): 201–17.

Loveman, Gary W. 1994. "An Assessment of the Productivity Impact of Information Technologies." In *Information Technology and the Corporation of the*

1990s, edited by Thomas J. Allen and Michael S. Scott Morton, 84–110. Oxford University Press.

Machlup, Fritz. 1992. *The Production and Distribution of Knowledge in the United States*. Princeton University Press.

McConnell, Sheila. 1996. "The Role of Computers in Reshaping the Work Force." *Monthly Labor Review* 119 (August).

Morrison, Catherine J., and Ernst R. Berndt. 1991. "Assessing the Productivity of Information Technology Equipment in U.S. Manufacturing Industries." Working Paper 3582. Cambridge, Mass.: National Bureau of Economic Research (January).

National Bureau of Economic Research. 1961. (The Stigler Report). *The Price Statistics of the Federal Government: Review, Appraisal, and Recommendations*. General Series 73. Cambridge, Mass.

National Research Council. 1994. *Information Technology in the Service Society: A Twenty-First Century Lever*. Washington: National Academy Press.

Nordhaus, William D. 1994. "Do Real Output and Real Wage Measures Capture Reality? The History of Lighting Suggests Not." Discussion Paper 1078. New Haven, Conn.: Cowles Foundation for Research in Economics.

Office of Management and Budget. 1987. *Standard Industrial Classification Manual*. U.S. Government Printing Office.

Oliner, Stephen D., and Daniel E. Sichel. 1994. "Computers and Output Growth Revisited: How Big Is the Puzzle?" *Brookings Papers on Economic Activity* 2: 273–317.

Organization for Economic Cooperation and Development (OECD). 1994. *Information Technology Outlook*. Paris.

Osterman, Paul. 1986. "The Impact of Computers on the Employment of Clerks and Managers." *Industrial and Labor Relations Review* 39 (January): 175–86.

Phister, Montgomery Jr. 1979. *Data Processing Technology and Economics*. Santa Monica, Calif.: Santa Monica Publishing Company.

Popkin, Joel. 1992. "The Impact of Measurement and Analytical Issues in Assessing Industry Productivity and its Relationship to Computer Investment," study by Joel Popkin and Company submitted to International Business Machines Corporation. Washington, D.C. (October).

Porat, Marc Uri. 1977. *The Information Economy: Definition and Measurement*. Office of Telecommunications, Special Publication 77-12 (May): 104–35. U.S. Department of Commerce.

Roach, Stephen S. 1991. "Services under Siege—The Restructuring Imperative," *Harvard Business Review* 68 (September–October): 82–91.

Romer, David. 1988. Comment on "The Productivity Slowdown, Measurement Issues, and the Explosion of Computer Power." *Brookings Papers on Economic Activity* 2: 425–28.

———. 1987. "Crazy Explanations for the Productivity Slowdown." *NBER Macroeconomics Annual*, edited by Stanley Fischer, 163–202. Cambridge, Mass.

Rostow, W. W. 1960. *The Stages of Economic Growth: A Non-Communist Manifesto.* Cambridge University Press.

Sichel, Daniel E. Forthcoming. "The Productivity Slowdown: Is a Growing Unmeasurable Sector the Culprit?" *Review of Economics and Statistics.*

Siegel, Donald. 1994. "Errors in Output Deflators Revisited: Unit Values and the Producer Price Index." *Economic Inquiry* 32 (January): 11–32.

Stiroh, Kevin. 1996. "Computers, Productivity, and Input Substitution." Working Paper. Bentley College, Waltham, Mass. (February).

Triplett, Jack E. 1989. "Price and Technological Change in a Capital Good: A Survey of Research on Computers." In *Technology and Capital Formation,* edited by Dale W. Jorgenson and Ralph Landau, 127–223. MIT Press

———. 1994. Comment on Oliner and Sichel, "Computers and Output Growth Revisited: How Big Is the Puzzle?" *Brookings Papers on Economic Activity* 2:318–24.

U.S. Department of Commerce, Bureau of the Census. 1975. *Historical Statistics of the United States, Colonial Times to 1970,* part 1 and part 2. Washington.

———. Bureau of Economic Analysis. 1992. *National Income and Product Accounts.* Washington.

———. 1993. *Fixed Reproducible Tangible Wealth in the United States, 1925–89.* Washington.

U.S. Department of Labor, Bureau of Labor Statistics. 1983. *Trends in Multifactor Productivity,* 1948–1981, Bulletin 2178 (September).

———. 1993. Multifactor Productivity Diskette.

———. 1996. *Detailed CPI Report:* 4–5.

Wilson, Diane D. 1993. "Assessing the Impact of Information Technology on Organizational Performance," In *Strategic Information Technology Management: Perspectives on Organizational Growth and Competitive Advantage,* edited by Rajiv D. Banker, Robert J. Kauffmann, and Mo Adam Mahmood, 471–514. Harrisburg, Pa.: Idea Group Publishing.

Willig, Robert, "Consumer Surplus without Apology." 1976. *American Economic Review* 66 (September): 589–97

Yates, JoAnne. 1989. *Control through Communication: The Rise of System in American Management.* Johns Hopkins University Press.

———. 1991. "Investing in Information: Supply and Demand Forces in the Use of Information in American Firms, 1850–1920." In *Inside the Business Enterprise: Historical Perspectives on the Use of Information,* edited by Peter Temin, 117–54. National Bureau of Economic Research and University of Chicago Press.

———. 1993. "Co-evolution of Information-Processing Technology and Use: Interaction between the Life Insurance and Tabulating Industries." *Business History Review* 67 (Spring) 1–51.

Yates, JoAnne, and Robert I. Benjamin. 1991. "The Past and Present as a Window on the Future." In *The Corporation of the 1990s: Information Technology and Organizational Transformation*, edited by Michael S. Scott Morton, 61–91. Oxford University Press.

Young, Allan H. 1992. "Alternative Measures of Change in Real Output and Prices." *Survey of Current Business* 72 (April): 32–48.

Yuskavage, Robert E. 1996. "Improved Estimates of Gross Product by Industry, 1959–94," *Survey of Current Business* 76 (August):150, table 10.

Zraket, Charles A. 1992. "Software: Productivity Puzzles, Policy Challenges." In *Beyond Spinoff: Military and Commercial Technologies in a Changing World*, edited by John A. Alic and others, 283–313. Harvard Business School Press.

Index